Stuck

City

E.D. Layton

Stuck City

Table of Contents

Dedication

To my Heavenly Father, Lord and Savior, who kept his hands on me throughout my journey. He loved me when I didn't love myself. To God be the glory.

To my beautiful daughters, I love you three so very much. I'm so proud of you. Thanks for staying strong In the Lord, not giving up on me, and praying me home. I also want to thank you for pushing me to finish this book.

To my niece, thank you for telling me I had a story to tell. It was hard re-living my pass, but I did it. Thank you so much. I love you

To my brothers, I want to thank you for your tough love when I needed it. Thank you for always being there for my daughters.

To my family, I love and adore you all for keeping your hands in my daughters lives. The Lord has truly blessed me with an awesome family.

Special Thanks

To my mother Areather and cousin Paulette, you both are beautiful, strong women and have done amazing jobs raising my daughters. I appreciate you with all my heart. Momma, please forgive me for every time I broke your heart. Paulette, you were an angel sent. I love you

To my Bishop L. Lawrence Brandon and Pastor Beryl Cowthran, I truly appreciate you. I thank God for using you to deliver lifesaving messages. I love you.

To Bishop Demetrius J. Sinegal, an awesome man of God and my son, & my daughter First Lady LaQuita Sinegal, words can't express how you have blessed me. Thanks for being patient with me. I appreciate all your help and time especially during this book writing process. I love you!

Foreword

Life has a way of writing its own story, and while everyone has a life, not everyone has the same story. What unifies us all, however, is that we all have a story that shares one underlying theme-LIFE HAPPENS!

If we are not careful not only will "life happen", but more Specifically LIFE will happen as the worst of things desire them to happen. The bible says" man that is born of a woman is of few days, and full of trouble," So this life that we are born into is destined to be filled with trouble, but the LIFE therein, is that you can have a new life, AFTER you have been born again.

Ms. Layton shares a powerful story about life, but more importantly shows us that being stuck is a choice. Life will certainly happen, and while it may be difficult to control what happens, you can control how you allow what has happened, effects you.

As a pastor, counselor, and life coach on a daily basis you encounter people who have been dealt a hand in life that at first does not seem favorable; but as you embark upon a behind the scenes view of life, Ms. Layton will show us that no matter how long you have been stuck where you are, you can ALWAYS get out, and

"change forward"

Bishop Demetrius J. Sinegal, Ph.D.

CEO -The Prophets House Publishing Company

Senior Pastor - The Kingdom Church

INTRODUCTION

The story you are about to read is true. My name is E. D. Layton, and I was born in Homer, Louisiana, raised in Compton, California. Growing up, I was squeaky clean, I never got into trouble or did anything illegal. I was, however, very out spoken and had what some people would call a mouth, a term used for people who always have a comeback or something to say to someone rather good or bad but most often perceived as a negative connotation. In my late twenties, I was introduced to rock cocaine and later became an addict.

My addiction led me to Skid Row, a dark, ugly and lonely place; no place for a woman. I was sick, lost and scared. I had to learn vastly to survive in the downtown streets of Los Angeles. I was full of shame which delayed my return home. During my time on Skid Row, I was beaten, robbed, and left for dead. I even had a personal date with the devil. After acclimating to Skid Row my second addiction became the "street life". Come read along the journey with me to see how life experiences can turn you upside down, but it's never too late to take control and begin altering your destiny. I would know, it took me 16 years to get it straight.

Today I have my life back, free from my drug addiction. Now I'm reunited with my family. Somehow I knew I would make it back home, but how would I and when. Here's my story....

Chapter One

It is the month of November, year of 1983. One afternoon after job hunting, my girlfriend Cindy came over to visit. She asked me to ride with her to a friend's house. I was really tired but decided to ride along. When we got in her car she said "Girl this guy is fine." I said, "Cindy, girl I know you're not trying to set me up?" She started to laugh and said no. Cindy was always trying to introduce me to someone. When we arrived, she knocked on the door and this dark skinny (fine as hell man) answered the door. Cindy didn't lie, he was fine. He asked us to come in, hugs Cindy said hello and then asked "Who is this lovely lady?" Cindy replied, "This is Dee, and Dee this is Bob." Bob said, "hello Dee" and led us into the den.

He offered us something to drink. Cindy handed Bob a twenty dollar bill, and said "give me a twenty". Bob walked to the other side of the room and came back with a plastic bag and handed it to Cindy. She then pulled out a

white rock. He looked at me and said "What about you?"
Cindy interjected, "She doesn't smoke, but she might want
to try it." I'm looking at Cindy wondering what the hell she
was talking about. Then, I saw her put a pipe to her mouth
and blow smoke out of it. While blowing the smoke out,
she had a soothing look on her face. By this time, Bob
hands me his pipe with a rock sitting on top. I waved my
hand saying no. Cindy said "Girl just try it, pull on it like a
cigarette, hold the smoke, then blow it out." So I did, and
they both started laughing at me. It seemed like a waste of
time because I didn't feel anything; so I didn't try it again. I
decided to just sit there and watch them.

After a while, I saw Bob looking at me as I was
looking at him. He had me really nervous, but in a good
way. Then he winked his eye; I couldn't help but blush. I
started feeling uncomfortable and told Cindy that I'm ready
to go. She said "in a moment." Bob interrupted her, and

11

asked me how long had I known Cindy? I told him since high school. He then started to ask personal questions, and asked me if I had a special man in my life? I told him no. I looked at Cindy and again told her I'm ready to go. She finally said o.k.

Cindy dropped me off at home. When I walked into the house, my brother Anthony mentioned to me that I got a call from Compton Unified School District and I have an interview on Tuesday. I remember that was on Thursday, and I was so happy that someone finally called me; I was tired of looking for work. On Tuesday, I interviewed with this very nice lady. She gave me the job and asked me to start the next day. Eagerly, I told her yes.

I couldn't believe they hired me at Jefferson Elementary the same day. I really enjoyed working at the elementary. Not long after I started working there, I met this guy named Donald, who worked for the school district as the school security guard. He was tall, handsome, and very funny. We begin to date and after talking to him six months, he asked me to marry him and I accepted. My mother was glad to hear I was

getting married. For some time, my mother had been waiting for me to meet someone and settle down. She always worried about me because I was a bit wild and ran the streets.

At the time I was proposed to, I still lived with my mother in South Gate, CA, along with my brother Anthony. (I have another brother Janatha but he moved out years ago). Donald and I were married on June 17th of 1984. I was twenty nine and he was thirty three. I really felt this was too soon, only six months knowing him, but I stepped out on faith hoping I made the right decision.

We were married in Las Vegas, and subsequently moved to Long Beach, CA. Six months later, my husband lost his job. One day while we were working at the elementary, he went to lunch with a friend, and allowed that friend to talk him into trying a street drug called PCP. He came back to work and started tripping. He took his clothes off and marched around the school yard. He got butt ass naked! The police came, took him off the school campus, and arrested him.

He was eventually fired and I was left in shame. He no longer had the means to take care of me or himself. What am I to do, I thought? Things took a turn for the worse. He started to drink, and we seemed to argue all the time. This was every day and it started to stress me out; I decided to get another job to make ends meet. I grabbed the first job that came along, which was selling Avon. Donald felt like he couldn't find a job, and to me it seemed like he had really given up. To make matters worse, three weeks after Donald lost his job they told me my job had ended, they no longer need me. Since everyone knew at work we were married, I believe they fired me due to the incident with Donald's arrest. Needless to say, at that point, I was really stressed out. I was not eating; losing weight, pulling my hair out, and cried all the time. I didn't know which way to turn and I considered giving up along with my husband. After a long talk with my mother, I decided to not give up, and worked on the problems in my marriage. I never told my mother how Donald lost his job. I was too embarrassed.

After struggling for the next month selling Avon, we end up moving to Oakland, CA. to live with my mother's sister aunt Lacy. She promised she would help us find jobs. My aunt and I were very close. Sometimes, I talked to her before I talked to my mother about my problems. I really missed my aunt Lacy when she moved from Los Angeles to Oakland, and I believed this move would be good for me.

My aunt kept her promise, and I landed a job working for Goodwill. However, my husband was having a hard time finding one. He drank all the time and I felt he didn't seem diligent in looking for work. It really made me anger. After being in Oakland two months, my husband called his brother in Baton Rouge, La. While on the phone, I overheard him say "man don't play" then laughed and said "o.k. I'll be there."When he got off the phone, he looked at me and said, "Baby, guess what? I got a job." "Where?" I said. He said, "In Baton Rouge., LA". I was astounded! I then thought to myself, oh Lord; I don't want to move to the country and so far away. But ultimately I did. I quit my job at the Goodwill, and like a nut moved to Baton Rouge with my husband. After all I did love him. I was sad because I didn't want to leave my aunt Lacy.

Surprisingly, once we were settled in Baton Rouge, things were really good and my husband started immediately working. The second week there, I received a letter from my aunt Linda. My aunt Linda had always been there for me. I quickly opened the letter; I was so happy to have gotten it. After reading my letter; I started to reminisce about her. One year, I got myself into some trouble, and she was there to help me out. After she helped me, she told me she knew just what I needed. So one Sunday morning, Aunt Linda took me to church. After church service, she looked at me and said, "Well did you like the service?" I said, "It was alright." She then said "Delores you never seem to amaze me (while laughing) with everything that has happen with you, I can write a book. I know it would be a bestseller." I said, "No, you won't Auntie because I'm not going to get into anymore trouble." She looked at me and said, "Delores your story has just begun."I didn't know what she was saying at that time, but I know now. My aunt was a sweetheart. I love, appreciate and miss her. Aunt Linda passed away in June of 1986 from breast cancer.

As days passed in Baton Rouge, it was too good to ask for my life to stay steady. To my surprise, my husband's brother smoked rock cocaine and we were soon trying to smoke too. Neither my husband nor I enjoyed it. Donald's thing was alcohol. For me, I never really felt anything. So I didn't understand the high, and I think I wanted to, so that's why I kept trying.

Once again, things really started to go downhill. My brother-in-law's girlfriend lived in the house as well, and she had a bad attitude. She would start to argue "just because." She would start a fight with my brother-in-law and say crazy things to me about my husband as if it was his fault in regards to their problems. I would get mad and start defending my husband, and that just made things worse. I soon grew tired of the mess and asked my husband to send me home. He looked at me and said "Baby we are at home." I replied "No, this is not home." He got angry at me and was reluctant to send me back, but he did.

When I got back to Los Angeles, I felt so relieved. A couple of weeks after getting home, I called an ex-boyfriend. I really can't say why, but perhaps it was because he was a good listener. I needed someone to talk to. After talking to him, I felt better and started to wonder if I got married too soon. But still, I was not ready to give up on my marriage. Later that week, I found out that I was pregnant. Now I had the task to call and tell my husband the news; we had a child on the way. Surprisingly, the day I told him, he was very happy. He told me he was still working and would be back soon.

Now months have passed, and Donald has lost his job with his brother. He decided to move to Montgomery, LA. with his mother, and there he found another job. Donald then sent for me. At this time, I was six months pregnant. Well, there I went on another road trip, and this time to Montgomery, LA., a place I never heard of, but again, I went to be with my husband. I made it there and immediately disliked everything about that place. It was more country than Baton Rouge. For the first week I was so unhappy, but I never expressed my feelings or concerns to anyone. I really didn't want to be there, and definitely didn't want to have my baby there. They went fishing every day and I couldn't go with them. I was so tired of hearing "pregnant women draw snakes". My everyday pastime was sitting on the porch. At least my mother-in-law was really sweet; she made sure I ate for my baby.

I didn't know how I was going to tell my husband I was unhappy living there, but I knew I needed to tell him. I waited a few weeks before I told him. Thinking maybe things would change, but they didn't. So one day, I got the courage and asked him to send me home. And oh my God, he was so angry. For two minutes he just stared at me, and then he said, "don't you want to make your home here?" I said "No! I need to be in the city, because I'm pregnant and I don't want to travel thirty miles to have my baby. Plus, I'm tired of dreaming about snakes. Maybe I should go back and have my baby; then come back. Donald please send me home." Once again he did and I felt bad for leaving him.

Chapter Two

I made it back to Los Angeles and moved back in with my mother. One month later on December 14th 1986, I gave birth to a beautiful baby girl. We named her LaQuita Vontrese, Donald gave her the name LaQuita and I named her Vontrese. Donald arrived one week after she was born as a proud father. Donald decided to stay with his sister, Fran, in Lynwood to spend some time with her. (We also lived with his sister a brief period after marriage before moving to Long Beach.) He told me after looking at his daughter that things would get better for us. He explained he was going to buckle down and find a job in Los Angeles. I believed him, and I believed he loved me.

But unfortunately, things did not get better. I began losing feelings for him and I finally realized we had gotten married to soon. Neither one of us were ready. We made a huge mistake getting married! Yet we had a beautiful baby together. I really believed he wanted to make it work, but didn't know how. For me, I didn't care anymore, but was trying to make it work for my baby. Maybe that was the wrong thing to do; it stressed me out trying to make it work.

One day my friend Cindy came over with some rock cocaine. She got me to try it again. Would you believe it, this time I liked it!! I finally felt the high; I was so relaxed, it seemed as if I had no problems. I felt good and numb. That night, I told Donald just how I felt. I told him, I thought we needed to separate before we went any further, that things were not getting better, but I needed him to be there for our baby. I explained that I felt this marriage had no foundation, and without a strong foundation nothing would ever securely stand. Thinking back, I can say he never gave up on us but I did.

Donald came over every day to see LaQuita after we separated. We argued constantly about any and everything all the time. I knew what it was, he wanted my attention, and I wasn't having it. I started to smoke a lot. One day, I decided to go to church, even though I was still smoking. I knew I needed some help. After I decided to start attending church services regularly, I decided to have LaQuita christened and I sung in the church choir.

At this point in my life, I was still staying with my mother and Donald was still in my life. You see it was hard saying no to Donald. One year and nine months later, I got pregnant again. By this time I was addicted to rock cocaine. I really tried to stop, but my addiction was too strong. The longest I could stop was one week. I remembered I always rubbed my stomach telling my baby to "please be strong for me, because mommy is not." I was really ,trying and found myself crying a lot with that pregnancy. Donald and I constantly fought but through all that I remained in church and sung in the choir.

One day Donald came over to the house, I asked Donald to go to the store to buy LaQuita some pampers. He said, "After you give me some." I replied, "I'm not going to have sex, man." Then he asked, "Why?" I told him I was too far in my pregnancy. He started pulling on me with LaQuita in my arms, saying "put LaQuita down". I said no, and he tried to take Quita out of my arms. I grabbed the nearest thing to me, which was a crystal vase, and hit him on the arm. He was surprised I hit him, but left and said he'll be back with the pampers but when he got back we were having sex. He took a while to come back and I had fallen asleep with LaQuita beside me in the bed. I woke up feeling something wet hit my face. I looked up and saw Donald ejaculating over me. I jumped up and forced him out of the house.

On September 6, 1988, I gave birth to another beautiful girl. I named her Raquel Lee. She was given her dad's middle name, and Donald was once again a proud father. The bad news was my baby was born with cocaine in her system. The doctors ran many test and only found a trace of cocaine once in her urine. Even with that news, I knew I was in huge trouble. It was good I stopped smoking the last week of pregnancy due to it making me sick. Thank God I got sick!!

When the social worker came in my room to talk to me; she told me that they would have to take my baby. Right away I started to cry. I asked her if my mother could take Raquel; she said yes as long as she signed the proper paperwork she could take her home but she would be essentially in her care. For this to be a messed up situation, I was very elated to know I would be able to be close to my baby. I definitely didn't want my baby to be in the foster care system and end up living in an unfamiliar area. This was my baby and I loved her. The mess I made almost cost me my child. I never thought I could be so weak, and so stupid!

After I was home with my baby for two months, trying to stop smoking, I decided to get some help. On December 2nd, 1988 I enrolled myself into a drug program, in the city of Norwalk, CA. I stayed there for eight months. I asked Donald to help my mother with the girls, while I was away. He did for a while and finally gave up and moved back to Montgomery, LA. When he left Raquel was five months. I guess he gave up on us, we were not getting along, but during that time I really needed him.

My stay in the program went well. My mother brought the girls to see me every week-end after the first sixty days. When I finished the program, I went back to church and enrolled in school to become a C.N.A. I finished and began working at a convalescent home in the city of Long Beach, CA. Years passed and I was blessed to find a pre-school right down the street from my place of employment. I remembering saving money for a car. We rode the city bus until I was able to get a car. I would drop the girls off in the morning; and when I got off work, we would walk to the bus stop and go home. {Thinking back, I remember telling my mother, that I don't want to put the girls in school until they could talk good enough to tell me if someone "mess" with them. I remember her looking at me and saying, "well they are ready". We both started laughing.}

One day on the bus back home with LaQuita sitting next to me, and Raquel on my lap. Raquel looked at me and said "Mommy, I want to be a nurse just like you, when I grow up." I told her o.k. Then LaQuita looked at me and said "Not me, I want to be a doctor because the nurse only does what the doctor says do." I was shocked but said o.k. I wondered how she knew that. When I got to the house, I called my husband to see how he was doing and to let the girls say hi. He told me that he was coming back. I wanted to say why, but I didn't.

Donald arrived in approximately one month after that phone call; I was so glad he decided to live with his sister. I was still working and in church with the girls. One day he was over to the house, playing with the girls and he stopped and looked at me. He was winking his eye and throwing kisses. I knew what he wanted; he wanted to have sex, but little did he know I was not going to give in to him. Donald began to mess with me and I fought him off which made things worse because he was angry. We started to argue and then he accused me of seeing someone. I laughed at him and he got even angrier. He began to get louder and louder and I told him he had to leave. I was not going to let my girls see us fight. Things really got worse for Donald and me. For the next eight months, things continued the same way. We could not get along. We argued about everything and sometimes we would fight. He was good for spending time with the girls. I just didn't know how long it would last before he decided to take off again.

Donald came over every day, which was a good thing for the girls. But for me, it stressed me out. I was tired of fighting with him. He would be at the house waiting for us when I got home from work. All the stress turned me to picking up a pipe. I knew I should have stopped him from coming over for good instead of allowing myself to get weak, but I didn't and soon found myself depending on the drug again. I started missing days from work and was eventually fired. I also stopped going to church.

I switched schools for the girls and enrolled them in a school near the house. I finally stopped Donald from coming to the house. However, he began to ignore my wishes and began to show up. The last time he showed up, we fought and argued because he could not have his way. This was the bottom line, he had to go. When Donald left that time, it was for good. He went back to live in Louisiana. (where he currently resides and works in the church as a minister). Later, Donald and I were divorced. Shortly after Donald left, I filed for welfare. I was able to go without any governmental assistance until that point.

Chapter Three

One Friday, the girls were looking at Beauty and the Beast. My cousins Annese and Clyde came over and we sat at the table playing dominoes. Later, my cousin Clyde asked me if I wanted to go with them over to his friend's house. I said, "Yes, but let me see if mommy feels like watching the girls." So I walked into my mother's room and ask her if she would watch the girls for a while. I would normally have them with me, but I knew there were no kids where I was going. My mother asked, "What time is it?" I told her and she said, "Yes, but get them ready for bed, before you leave." Then she said, "They might not let you leave (trying to be funny)." We both started laughing.

I turned off the T.V. and got them ready for bed. When I headed towards the door, they wanted to know where I was going. They started to cry and wanted to go with me. It was hard saying no to them but they were always with me. I told them not to cry; tomorrow their

34

cousins, Tonisha and Marcus, were coming over and we're going to the park. I also let them know I wouldn't be gone long. They went for it; I kissed them and left. As I walked out the door I heard my mom shout, "Lock the door."

When we got to his friend's house, we played cards. After playing, we sat around telling jokes. On the way home, I asked Clyde to make a stop. I told him that I wanted something to smoke. He said, "Stop where?" Then Annese said, "Clyde, you know where, this is your side of town. And you know everyone". Now Annese didn't smoke, her thing was drinking beer; she just spoke up for me. So Clyde said, "O.k. I hope this guy still lives here. " I said "who?" and he said, "AM PM, that is what they call him."

So Clyde pulled up to this house and parked. He got out and said, "I'll be right back". I knew Clyde really didn't want to knock on the door because he didn't do drugs but Clyde always had our backs; he would do anything for us. When Clyde came back from inside the house, oh my God; he had this tall, handsome guy, with a big smile and a deep voice walking alongside him. I could here them talking on their way to the car. It was love at first sight for me. I knew I was crazy and needed to stop; I just got out of a marriage not too long ago. While we were watching them walk towards us, Annese was trying to ask me something about the guy, but they were already at the car before I could understand what she was saying. The guy said hello and then asked me what I wanted. He asked me to get out the car and go in the house with him. So I did and Annese was right behind me.

My eyes were set on this man; it was crazy. I remember Annese saying "Dee this man is fine," and I said, "He sure is." When we were in the house, he gave me what I wanted with a smile. And that was it; I had to get to know him. He left out the room and just as we were leaving, he walked back into the room and asked me my name and wanted to know if he could have my phone number. I told him, "Dee, and yes" and proceeded to give him my number. On the way home, I talked about him; I asked Clyde all kinds of questions. Since, he didn't tell me his name and I forgot to ask, I had to ask Clyde his name. Clyde said his name was Paul. I didn't know at that time, but Paul would be my next child's father.

When I made it home, the girls were asleep. The next morning, when I got up, the girls were awake and they asked me what time their cousins were coming over; they wanted to go to the park. I got up and cooked breakfast, and by then Tonisha and Marcus were at the door knocking, with my brother Anthony. We ate, I got them dressed, combed their hair and we went to the park. I let them play until they were tired. When we got back, I gave them a sandwich and some Kool-Aid and they fell asleep on the floor watching the television.

A little later that day, Paul called and we talked for hours. The next day, he asked to come over; I told him that he could come over after church. So that Sunday, he came over after church, and we sat around talking. This went on for months, five months later, we became a couple. We got along good together; I enjoyed his company. At that point, I was still getting high. Paul didn't get high, but since he sold being with him made it easier to get my drugs but there were times when he said no. Paul and I were together 11 months before I got pregnant.

On August 12th of 1994, I gave birth to another baby girl. Sad to say, but I had another girl born with cocaine in her system. We named her Erika Tiffany Nacolsha. I allowed the girls to name their sister. LaQuita named her Tiffany, Raquel named her Nacolsha (I remember asking her twice saying, "baby do you mean Nicole;" she said "no momma),"

and I named her Erika from her father Paul Eric. Erika was the largest of my babies; she weighed 7 1/2 pounds. LaQuita weighed 5 1/2 pounds and Raquel was 6.6 pounds.

Before I went into labor, I gave my girls specific instructions on what to do when my water broke, and I must say they did exactly how we rehearsed. LaQuita went next door to get my neighbor because my phone was off. (I allowed my phone bill to get high with Paul calling from jail.) Raquel went into the bedroom and got my purse and coat. I remember she looked down and saw the water on the floor, where my amniotic sack had broken, and said, "Mommy look at all that pee, did you pee on yourself." I responded "No, that's just water." Then she asked, "Where did it come from?" I immediately told her to go find her sister.

While I was in the hospital, I did a lot of thinking about my life. One thing was how I was going to tell my babies their mommy had to go away. I knew once again I had to get myself some help and fast before I lost my girls. The only person I could think of to watch my girls was my cousin Paulette. She was always at my mother's house before I moved out into my own home. She would came over on Sundays after church and after bible study during the week. We were very close, she was a good person, and I knew I could trust her with my girls.

I don't know how it happened, but I left the hospital with my baby knowing she was born with cocaine in her system. Later, a social worker found me and came out to my house to talk to me. She told me if I didn't get myself into a program or get myself together, I was going to lose my girls. She expressed, "I should take them now, but I know you will do the right thing Mrs. Layton, here's my number if you need to talk." She gave me a time and date when she would be back. Right away I called Paulette. I had grown comfortable always having my mother to lean on and pick up the pieces but this time my mother had remarried and moved to Haynesville, LA. Since Paul was busted for selling drugs, I didn't have him either.

I called Paulette and explained my situation. I remember telling her I needed her help and asked if she would watch the girls until I got myself together. I expressed to her how important it was for me to go into a drug program before I lost my girls. I conveyed, "If you decide to help me please call my mother or brother Janatha if any problems occur that prevents you from keeping the girls any longer. Please don't let my babies go to a foster home. I love my girls, but need some help." Paulette said she would help me. When I finished talking to her, she prayed with me. After talking to Paulette, I called the social worker. I told her that I was going back into a drug program and my cousin would be taken the girls.

The social worker was scheduled to be back out to the house in three weeks, and she would be taking my girls to live with Paulette. Now I had the assignment to sit my girls down and talk to them. I called the girls in from outside playing and asked them if it would be alright for me to go back to school. LaQuita said, "Why mommy? You didn't go to school when you were a little girl?" I said, "Yes baby, mommy wants to go back to school to learn how to become a good mother." She said, "You are a good mother." So I said, "a better mother." Then Raquel said, "Are you going to school like me mommy?" I told her "No, I will have to stay a while." She asked, "For how long?" I said, "six months." Raquel said, "No mommy that's too long."Now I know my baby didn't know how long six months actually was, but I guess it six months seemed like a long time. After my eyes were filled with tears, LaQuita looked up at me, and said, "Mommy you want to go to school?" I said, "Yes."Then she said, "OK mommy you can go to school, don't cry" and began to wipe the tears that fell from my face. Raquel began to wipe my tears as well but she kept saying, "No mommy."

Later that night after the girls were sleep, I laid down and thought about how I missed my mother. I was mad because she left me, but I knew she had her own life to live and I had to grow up. The more I thought about my situation, I knew I had only myself to blame. I told myself this time, I was going to make a change. I was not willing to lose my girls.

Three weeks had passed and the social worker has arrived to take the girls. I really thought, I was ready for that day, but I wasn't. The girls were crying and didn't want to go. I was crying even harder. They would not let go of me, I hugged them while telling them it's alright, and they were going to stay with Paulette. The social worker attempted to pull them from me which made me get angry. I stopped her and explained that I would get them to go with her. When they started to let go, I knelt down and told them not to cry. I expressed how much I loved them, for them to be good girls for me, and to listen to Paulette. Then I told LaQuita to take care of her sisters and to make sure they remained best friends. Before I kissed them goodbye, I promised that I would write and call them. Then I picked up Erika, looked into her big eyes held her tight and gave her a kiss goodbye. After they were gone, I cried so hard. I cried for the rest of that day. I remember waking up with a headache feeling so lost.

Approximately a week later, September 1994, I went into the drug program, Safe Harbor. Getting on the bus, I remember thinking of my girls and how I missed them. I knew I was doing the right thing; I had an addiction

and could no longer take care of them in with that state of

mind. Walking into the building, I felt good about myself

and my decision, not realizing what lied ahead of me.

Chapter Four

For the first time, I really felt good about myself; however, I could not talk to my family for the next thirty days. After my initial thirty day detox, my cousin Sally came to visit me. She brought me some clothes and personal hygiene products. I was so happy to see her. I thanked her for the clothes and asked about my girls. She said they were good and missed me. So after she left, I called them. It felt so good hearing their voices. They were happy to hear from me. I asked what they had been doing, told them I love them and will see them soon. Then I got off the phone before I started to cry. My girls and I were always together, and it was hard being away from them. I thought about leaving to go see them, but I knew I had too much to lose.

The next morning in one of my classes, this girl and I got into an argument. I tried to ignore her, but she kept getting in my face calling me names; so we began to fight. This ended in both of us being kicked out of the program. I was told to pack my bag and leave right away. Before I left, my counselor told me that I could come back after 90 days. She then said good luck. 'Good luck', was she for real, what am I going to do now? I walked out the door and found myself on the streets of Skid Row. I had no street knowledge, and I didn't know anyone. There was one thing I did know and that was my family could not find out. I knew they would be hurt and disappointed in me. So, I made up my mind not to call anyone or go home until I got back into the program.

I remember standing outside Safe Harbor, wondering which way to start walking. I began walking down Fifth Street. The streets were filled with people. I saw many tents set up on both sides of the street. There were men winking their eyes at me and women rolling their eyes at me. What have I got myself into, I remember thinking. I saw men on their knees shooting dice; two men were fighting. Some people were sitting up against the wall eating; some sleep. I saw some smoking dope and drinking. People were even dancing in the street. To me, it seemed like a wild block party. I continued to walk onto another street and it was also full of people. As I continued to walk, I began to grow fearless; my fear had begun to turn into curiosity. I heard of homeless people, but I didn't know this was how they lived. I definitely had no idea this place would become my home for another decade and a half.

I began to grow tired walking, so I stopped to take a break and sat on some steps. Then this girl hollered from across the street saying, "I know you don't think you're going to come over here and make my money bitch." Then she started to cross the street over to me. She said, "Bitch where you come from?" I said, "Why are you calling me a bitch? You don't know me." By that time a man came over to us from across the street and said, "You need to chill Jello." He then said hi to me and asked me my name. I told him Dee and he asked, "Did you just touch down?" I asked, "What?" (I didn't know what touch down meant.) He said, "Are you just getting out of jail? I have never saw you before and you are pretty thick." I said, "No I just left a program." He said, "Oh you mean Safe Harbor?" I answered, "Yes." Then he wanted to know what city I was from; I told him Compton. He asked, "If I was on my way home?" I responded, "No, I just stopped to rest after my long walk." He said, "This is not a good place to rest. This is the hoe stroll. Let's walk over here so you can rest a while."

I got up and we walked across the street to this big open lot where a tent was sitting. Then the girl he called Jello said, "Okay you're doing the right thing Tony, you better take that bitch somewhere before she gets a beat down, coming here trying to make my money." I looked at Tony and said, "What's her problem?" He said, "You are a new face around here, you look good, and you have a nice body. She is jealous and feels threatened by you." Then he looked at me up and down and said, "Girl, you really do have a nice body." I began to get scared all over again. I knew I needed to get up and leave; so I told him it was getting late and I need to go.

I started walking not knowing where I was headed. I continued to walk, thought of my girls, and started to cry. I wiped my tear, looked up and saw a phone booth thoughts of calling them ran through my mind. I then saw a girl sitting on the sidewalk next to a tent. When I reached her at the tent, she said, "Hi do you have a lighter?" I said yes and gave her a light. Then she asked me the same question Tony asked me, which was did you just touch down? Only this time I knew what to say. "I just left a program; actually, I was put out for fighting." She said, "Look on the other side of the tent and get a crate to sit on." She added, "I know that bag is heavy." I replied, "Yes it is!" She said, "Sit it down over here." She asked me my name. I said, "Dee, and Your name?" "Call me Little Bit," she replied. She followed with, "Oh I don't mean to be rude, but do you smoke?" I answered, "Yea, but I'm cool." Then she asked where I was going. I don't know was my response. Little bit said, "You can stay here with me until you figure it out, that's if you want to."

I asked her how long she had been down here. "Seven years," she replied. "What! Are you kidding me,"I said. She said, "Yes girl, I have been down here a long time and you should hurry from down here because you don't want to get hung up. This is no playground and people here are no joke. Please don't get hung up, it is so easy to do." I asked her why she was down here. She said it was not by choice. So I asked, "What do you mean?" She said, "My husband worked for Amtrak train station, and one day on his way home from work, he got off the bus and started walking home; some shots were fired and he was shot in the head. The same night he died. The next day I just packed a bag and left my home and everything I owned. I ended up out here. It just didn't seem right to live without him in our home we built together."

I wanted to know why she said it wasn't by choice, but I didn't ask (I felt her pain). She looked at me and said, "Dee did I give up on life?" But before I could answer her, she stated, "So here I am and you should go home. Please go home Dee." I responded, "I will after I get back into the program and finish. I hadn't told my family what happened and I miss my girls so much but I cannot seem to call them." She said, "Call them. I'm sure they will understand." "Oh no, my girls are too young," I explained.

She said, "No I mean your family." "Well, my family might understand, but I feel like I have let them all down. I'm going to wait until I'm back in the program. I just don't know what I'm going to do until then." "What you need to do is call your girls. I told you that you can stay here with me."

"Do you have money because you can get a room?" asked Little Bit. That reminded me that I needed to find the G.R. building. I told Little Bit I needed to go there so I could get my checks changed over in my name. When I was in the program I had to sign my checks over to the program to pay for my stay there. I explained, "I need to have my checks switched over this month or my check will go to the program." Little Bit said, "Don't worry, Dee I will take you there." "Tell me Little Bit, where do you use the bathroom." She started to laugh, and said, "At McDonalds because the mission is too far and McDonald's is open 24 hours. Do you have to use the bathroom Dee? It is right on the corner." I replied, "Oh no, I just wanted to know where would I go."

Little Bit began telling me that it wasn't going to be easy out here and there were people out here that will hurt me. She started by saying, "I've learned over the years being here that they are serious about their money. It's all about them hustling. They have no heart; it's all about them. They care about nothing. Just their money and dope; you can't trust anybody. You will have to learn who is who. One way you will learn them is by listening to their conversation. Listen Dee, they have killers and rapists down here. Some are just out here to jack you. You never talk to the police or anyone who is asking questions. You never give any information out. And if you have a warrant, don't carry your ID. To keep money, you will need a hustle. Nobody will give you anything and you don't want them to because there will be a price to pay. (trust that) Dee if you get into a fight you better fight back, win or lose, you will gain their respect. But if you don't fight back, you will seem weak to them and they will pick on you until you fight them back. And believe me Dee, they are going to test you. I'm not trying to be funny, but I don't think this place is for you baby girl. I can tell you have a good heart. And your tears let me know that you really want to go home. I bet you have a family somewhere who loves you and wants you home. Oh Dee, don't ever flash your money. You never know who is watching you. Dee you really need to go home. I'm telling you these are true gangsters out here with no heart and they will not care about hurting you. Now, there is some out here with a hearts, but very few. Don't get mixed up with the whores down here, they really can't be trusted, or the pimp's. The women are more dangerous than the men. But the men have more unity than the women.

This is sad, right Dee, because the women really have it hard down here, and we really need to stick together."

Now, she got me scared all over again, but I'm not going home yet until I finish what I started. "Dee I have to use the bathroom, will you be alright?" I answered, "Sure!" When she left, I was there thinking about everything she told me. I went inside her tent; I wanted to see what it looked like, and I even smelled her blankets to see if they were clean, and everything was clean. I needed to know since I was going to be sleeping there because I really didn't want to go to a hotel just yet. I needed to hold on to my money, plus I didn't feel safe going to a hotel. Little bit seemed like a caring person, and I needed to know someone. I remembered her saying, "trust no one," so I took my money out of my purse, which was in my bag, and placed it in my panties. I had to be safe because I just met her. There was something telling me that I could trust her.

The truth is she didn't have to share all of what she did share in regards to the street life.

I hadn't eaten all day so I decided to walk to McDonald's. I saw Little Bit and I got something to eat; we walked back to her tent together. When we got back, there was a man sitting outside her tent waiting for her. She saw him, and said "there's my customer; I know just what he wants, right on time. He wants to spend forty dollars." My mouth dropped open; I had no idea she sold dope. I walked straight in the tent to eat my food. After I finished eating, I started going outside but Little Bit beat me as she was coming inside. I asked her for a twenty rock and we smoked it together. We continued to talk about street life, and soon we both fell off to sleep.

The next morning we got up and she showed me the mission, where we took a shower. I asked her how much the shower would cost? She laughed and said, "Dee it's free, and you can make a phone call to your girls." But I didn't call the girls at that time. As we were walking to go eat breakfast, Little Bit said, "And it's free!" She was still laughing at me and said, "You have a lot to learn." When we sat down to eat, I looked around and could not believe all the women I saw in there. After eating on the way back to the tent, I looked around and this guy seemed to be following us. So I said something to Little Bit, and she looked back and said, "Oh he is harmless. He does this all the time. His name is Thomas. He was a songwriter but then something happened to him and his family. Girl I don't know the whole story but I guess he just gave up on life. I'm guessing, whatever it was he couldn't handle it. I believe it just took his mind because he talks to no one. Dee you would be surprised who is down here. There's people from all walks of life. If you can survive out here you can make it anywhere. Girl, I tell you this is the school of hard knocks and a living hell." I said to myself, I'm going to the program soon so I can get home. (I didn't know at this time that I will soon be out here in the streets marching with the devil. And the girl, that is teaching me the street life will soon die.)

When we were back at the tent Little Bit told me that she had to go and meet this truck driver. She asked if I would be alright and that she wouldn't be long. I said, "Yes I will be alright." After she left, I sat outside the tent and I thought about my situation, and how long I had before I could go to the program. I looked up and saw that girl named Jello coming down the street. I watched her until she was in my face, saying "What's up bitch?" She asked what was I doing sitting in front of Little Bit's tent. I answered, " waiting for her." She then said, "Bitch, you gotta get up out of here. I believe you're trying to steal something." So I stood up and said, "What?", and before I could say anything else she hit me and I fell back against the wall. She kept hitting me, I didn't have a chance to hit back or get to my feet. Then she left me laying there. I tell you she beat my butt. All I could do was pick myself up and go inside the tent.

When Little Bit came back I told her what happen. She was so mad and said, "See Dee, I told you they were going to test you. Did you fight back?" I told her that she caught me off guard. "Hell I didn't have a chance to fight back. And she was real fast. I could not get up." She looked at me and said, "Now you want to go home." I said, "No not yet." She just shook her head and laughed.

The next day Little Bit took me to the G.R. building, the general relief government building. After changing my checks back into my name, we stopped back by the store to buy some cigarettes. Leaving out of the store we saw a man in an eighteen wheeler. So she went to the truck and I waited on her. While I was waiting for her a man walked up to me and said, "Hi if I give you fifty dollars will you eat my boo-boo." I thought to myself, that I must have misunderstood him. I asked him, "What did you say?" So he said it again. I can't believe this, I got mad and responded sarcastically "If you eat mine first." And he said, "O.k." I covered my mouth and nose with my hand and took off running. I didn't even look back.

I kept running until I heard Little Bit call my name. I stopped and she asked me what was wrong? "Why are you running?" I told Little Bit what happen and she said, "Are you kidding me" and laughed. "Dee, I told you there are all kinds of people down here" as she continued to laugh. She said "Girl when I first got down here this man ask me if he could suck my toes. But I never had anyone ask me to eat his boo boo. He really is sick." On the way back to the tent, I wondered how Little Bit had lasted for seven years.

When we got back to the tent we started to smoke and after what just happen to me, I felt like I needed a drink, and I don't even drink. After we finished smoking, we sat outside the tent and a big truck pulled up across the street from the tent. This man motions his hand for her to come here. Little Bit said, "See what he want Dee." I said, "What, no you see." She said, "Dee you need to be learning what to do and you don't have to do anything you don't want to do. I will sit right here and watch you." So, I went and he wanted some dope. I told him to wait one minute and I told Little Bit. She went to the truck and served him. When she walked back to the tent, we sat in the tent and smoked some more.

We later sat outside the tent, a car pulled up and again a man motioned to come here. I walked to the car, but was looking back at Little Bit. She was laughing at me saying, "Go ahead scary cat." I shook my head while laughing. When I approached the car, this man said, "Hi you can get in." I really wasn't sure what to do, but I got in. This man asked me my name. I told him Dee. He said his name was Mike and asked if I partied. Before I answered him, there was a car that pulled up behind us, then another one in front of us. I didn't know what was going on. I was scared, and then this man opens my door and said I was being arrested for suspicion of prostitution. I looked over at Little Bit and she had her head down. I was so frightened. They took me to jail and I was booked for three days.

The good thing about me going to jail was I broke down and called my mother. It felt good hearing her voice. She told me that she had my girls and they were well, but missed me. She asked, "Why are you in jail?" Lord knows I couldn't tell my mother that the police arrested me for suspicion of prostitution. In which, I didn't understand myself because I didn't do anything. I lied and told her for drugs. I told her that I love her and my girls. "Mommy be sure to kiss the girls for me." I told my mother I was going to clean up this mess I had made of my life. Before I hung up the phone, my mother asked me what happen with the program. I really didn't want to tell her, but I had to. She asked, "Why were you fighting?" I didn't answer and was so ready to get off the phone. I didn't say much after that, but the truth was out and it felt good even though I was ashamed.

Leaving jail, I had to walk back to Seventh Street from First Street, and the blocks were long. On my walk back, all I could think about was me and how I didn't want to go home until I finished the program. I didn't want to let my girls down and I didn't want my family to be disappointed with me. I just needed to get back into the program.

When I got back to Seventh Street, I saw Little Bit sitting outside the tent. She looked up and saw me coming, got up and started to walk hurriedly towards me. She gave me a big hug and said, "Dee I'm so sorry, I forgot to tell you to ask if they were a police, and not say anything about money, until you are sure who they are." I told her that there was no money mentioned and I didn't do anything wrong. I was just talking. She said, "Oh they got you for suspicion of prostitution right?" I said "yes." "Well, Dee they got you because you got into the car. So that is called suspicion which is something we have to talk about." I said, "Oh no, because this will not happen again. Going to jail is not for me." Little Bit, said, "Girl, if you stay down here, it will happen again." She asked if I wanted a hit. I answered her so fast saying yes, she laughed. Then we went inside

the tent and we smoked.

Chapter Five

Later that day I left Little Bit in the tent and walked to the store to get some cigarettes. On the way back to the tent this guy hollered at me, saying, "girl you are wearing them pants." I didn't say anything I kept walking, but I heard this girl behind me say, bitch. I figured she was saying it towards me because of the attention I received from the guy. So I kept walking but I still heard her behind me talking crazy and starting to get louder. Then once again she called me a bitch, so I stopped and turn around. I stared directly in her eyes with a mean face letting her know I was not afraid of her.

She walked up to me and I knew I had to fight her because she was in my face. I really didn't want to fight, but the street was full of people looking. I remembered Little Bit saying they will test you. She kept pushing up on me and I had a flashback of Jello beating me up. Before I knew it, I hit her in her mouth and it was on. I kept hitting her; blood was everywhere. Blood was even on me but it wasn't my blood. When it was over, I heard people saying, "Who is that? Damn. She beat her ass. That's what she gets always messing with people. She should know that no one wants that man. I bet she go sit down now." I really felt bad, but walked away with my head held high.

On the way back to the tent, I started thinking about the girls and how much I really missed them. The fight I just had was behind me. I saw a phone booth and decided to call them. My mother answered the phone and she put them on and the girls were so happy and so was I. Just hearing their voices put a smile on my face. I told them that I love them, I would be home soon, and to be good for grandma.

After the phone call I walked on to the tent. Just as I got to the tent I saw this truck driver. He motions me to come here. I went to the truck and this man said, "Hello, get in." I said "no" (Thinking to myself 'hell no'). He began to talk, but I interrupted him by asking questions like how long had he been driving trucks, and was he married. I assumed this man was tired of me asking so many questions. He reached into his pocket and pulled out forty dollars and gave it to me then said, "have a nice day." He rolled up his window and drove off. I know he saw the blood on my shirt, but he didn't say anything.

I headed to the tent and there was Little Bit sitting by the tent. When I reached her, Little Bit said, "I saw you at that truck, but girl it looks like you been in a fight." I told her about the fight. She was proud because I stood up for myself. She said, "Dee you look like a fighter, but it takes a lot to make you fight. I was worried about you for a minute, but I can see you are going to be alright." I then told her about the truck driver and how I asked him a lot questions in which eventually he got tired of answering me and gave me forty dollars then left. She said, "Ok Dee, you have a gift of gab." She started laughing and then said, "Dee I guess that ass beating Jello gave you made you a soldier." I said, "I guess," and we both began laughed.

"Let's take a hit", Little Bit said. "You look like you need one and take off that bloody top." While we were in the tent smoking, she said, "Dee it's good you had that fight. Now they know you're not afraid of them and they won't test you. Well, not the ones that seen you fight. I can see you feel bad, but you should not feel bad; not at all, it's you or them. It's do or die." I heard someone call Little Bit's name. It was Jello. So Little Bit went out of the tent to see what she wanted. I stayed inside the tent changing my top. Jello told Little Bit she heard I had a fight, and asked her what happened. Little Bit told her I had a fight and was alright, and she should be asking the girl I had the fight with. "I heard she beat her down," Jello said, "where is she?" So Little Bit called me out the tent. As I walked out, I said, "What?" and then Jello said, "Good for you Dee. I'm sorry for what I did to you, but I had to see what you were made of. That's how we do things down here. Girl, keep your head up." Then she shook my hand and said see you later. I couldn't believe what had just happened.

Little Bit said, "See Dee, you are going to be alright. Let's take another hit and then come take a walk with me." So we did just that and walked to the back of the Texaco gas station on Alameda Street. The street was full of people. They walked around doing their thing. I noticed a man on the corner; I found out he was there to call out "one time" when he saw a police car coming their way. As we passed the people they were staring at me, but speaking to Little Bit. As we sat down on this cement porch off the ground aguy walked up to Little Bit and asked her if she had something. She said, "Yes. What do you want?" The guy said, "I want a twenty." She said, "Ok, give your money to Dee." He responded, "This pretty lady." I looked up very surprisingly when she said that to him. He gave me the money and she gave him the dope. He looked at me and said, "My name is slim." I said, "hi slim." Then I gave the money he gave me to Little Bit. He walked away but kept looking back at me. Little Bit said, "He'll be back. Dee don't pay him no mind; he is no good."

There was another guy who came wanting a ten so Little Bit said the same thing, give the money to Dee, and she served him. I realized doing this with Little Bit, they were learning my name. This went on for an hour. She had made three hundred dollars. So now I'm thinking, this might just be for me. I looked at Little Bit and told her I wanted to sell dope. She said "Dee this is why I got you out here with me, so you can see how it's done. Now look, you always sit in the middle of the street, so you can see the police on both ends of the street before they get to you. That way you have time to put your dope up. I put the dope sack in my mouth until the police pass me. Some people tuck it in their pants, some in the zipper of their pants, and some just throw it down not too far from them. So it won't be on them. Oh Dee, if you don't see a corner man make sure you call out ONE TIME if you see the police coming." Then she asked, "Where would you keep your dope?" I said, "I don't know let me think about it." She said, "Don't think too long because the next sell is yours." I said, "What!" and she said, "Girl you are ready." I responded, "I guess, and I will keep my dope in my hair." She responded, "Where Dee?" I said, "In my hair. I can tuck it in my ponytail next to my rubber band." She said, "Girl that's good. Here's the dope Dee and I will take the money. I won't always be with you so you will have to trust yourself and watch your own back. Don't let everyone walk up on you. Don't let them make a crowd around you because that draws attention to you. The police will then know you have the dope. You have to be careful and not get distracted. You will learn as you go. Tell your customers to always have their money ready before they get to you. You don't want them coming up to you counting their money. Get ready, here comes your first sell."

I looked up at her and asked, "Little Bit one rock is five dollars right?" She said, "Yes, but if they ask for a twenty I give them five for twenty." This guy walked up to Little Bit and asked for a twenty. Little Bit said, "She got the rocks; pass me your money." He looked at me then back at Little Bit, and said, "You don't have anything?" "Yes," Little Bit replied, "but I have Dee selling for me." So he asked if he still gets five for twenty. Little Bit answered yes with a laugh. He gave her his twenty dollar bill and I gave him five rocks. He said, "Thank you, what's your name?" I said Dee. He turned and left but then turned around and said, "Hey Dee I'll be back." I looked at Little Bit and smiled. I did this for about forty five minutes and we left. Little Bit said she didn't like to be in one spot too long.

As we were walking, Little Bit bent over holding her stomach. "Are you alright?" I asked. She started to throw up so I put the bag of dope in my hair, put my hand on her back and asked her again. I could see that she wasn't. She looked at me and said, "Dee let's go." I helped her up and asked her if she wanted some water? She said, "Yes." I didn't want to leave her, but I ran to the front of the gas station. I got back with the water, and we sat there for a few minutes. On the walk back to the tent, I asked her what was wrong with her again. She said, "Nothing, I'm alright Dee." "Little Bit, you just don't throw up for nothing." She said, "Leave it alone." So I left it alone until we got back to the tent. When we got back to the tent, I looked at her and said, "So you're not going to tell me what's wrong with you?" She said, "Dee please don't worry about me, I do this all the time. I think I have an ulcer. Believe me girl I'm alright." She changed the subject and said, "Dee you did good, let's count the money. Why don't you finish selling, for me today? You can sit right outside the tent."

For the little time I was out there selling for her, I made one hundred and sixty five dollars. Before the day had ended, I made five hundred and sixty five dollars, but I was up until 2 am. My mind was really on Little Bit. I checked on her from time to time and she slept the whole time. I didn't know why but I felt there was something really wrong with her. She really looked bad to me. The stuff she had thrown up was yellow.

When we woke up that morning, I gave her the money I made last night. She was so surprised, she handed me two hundred dollars. I said, "No that's o.k. I wanted to sell for you." She said, "Dee don't do work for anyone for nothing, not even me. If you get caught with the dope, selling for someone else, you will do the time in jail." So I decided then if I'm going to sell dope, I will do it myself; this will now be my hustle. I told Little Bit thank you and she said for what? "For being here for me, because if it were not for you I would really be lost out here," I said. She said, "Thanks Dee for being a friend. I think we needed each other." I said, "Yes we made a pretty good team yesterday." She said, "If anything should happen to me Dee, I mean if I ever got busted and go to jail, I want you to stay here in my tent and be strong. And remember trouble will come your way. Trust no one. Please depend on yourself." She really had me worried after that last spill, but I just said okay.. She asked me if I prayed. I said, "Yes for my girls, my mother and family." "Good keep praying Dee, but pray for you too." I said, "I sure will Little Bit."

I asked if she was hungry, then walked to McDonald's to get us something to eat. When I got back, she was sitting outside the tent talking to this guy. So I gave her, her food and went inside the tent to eat. I was so hungry and still sleepy; I ate and took a short nap. I woke up with my girls on my mind and began to pray. "Heavenly Father, please watch over my girls, let them know that I love them. I know their hearts hurt and miss me. I know they don't understand why I'm not with them. Please help them and keep them safe. Watch over my mother and my family. Please don't let them give up on me, and Lord please help me get home. In Jesus name Amen." Man, I love them so much. But I knew I did the right thing, by trying to get help. I knew they were better off with my mother at that time. I started to cry and heard Little Bit tell the guy she was talking to she would see him later, so I dried my eyes.

After Little Bit came back into the tent, we walked to the Mission to take a shower. When I was in the shower line to get a towel, Little Bit asked, "Do you ever wonder why these women are down here?... Life." I then said, "Maybe bad decisions." Again she said, "Life! life put us here Dee." I don't know what to believe anymore. All I know is if I wasn't so ashamed I would be home. I wish I could face my family. I missed my girls and my family. The time is going by so fast, but not fast enough. I wanted to get back into the program. I questioned myself, asking why I ran to drugs. I knew I had to find myself fast because my girls needed me and I needed them.

After we showered, we went to the tent and the same guy that was there this morning was sitting outside the tent. Before we got to the tent Little Bit said, "Oh Dee, Rob wanted to meet you, but you were eating and fell asleep. I think this is why he's back." I said, "What!?" and stopped mid-sentence because we were at the tent. We both

said, "Hey." He said, "You must be Dee, with a big smile."

I said, "Yes, what is your name?" Even though I already

knew his name, but didn't know what else to say. He said,

"Rob." I got the other crate and sat beside him and we

started to talk. I remember asking him how long he had

been in the street. He told me since 1975. I could not

believe what I was hearing, that's a long time! We

continued to talk until Little Bit called me into the tent. She

wanted to know if I wanted to get some dope for myself to

sell. I said, "Yes, but am I ready?" She said, "Girl I think

you are." So I said okay. Little Bit said, "Tell me when Rob

leave and we can go, and Dee he's no good either,"

pointing outside the tent. Then she said, "Ask Rob if he

wants anything." I asked him and he said, "no, not now.

Tell her maybe when I get back." As Rob and I continued

to talk, he revealed that he sold dope from time to time. We conversed for another twenty minutes and he left.

Shortly after, Little Bit and I left to get the bag of dope for me to sell. I really didn't know at this time, but I was about to gain another addiction, which was street life. Yes my lifestyle became another addiction. We walked to 5th street to meet her connection. There were a lot of people out there buying and smoking drugs. There were many people standing along the street begging but most of them were selling. Little Bit spots her guy looked at me and asked for fifty dollars. She said he was going to give her a double up, which means he's going to give her more for her money. Little Bit told me to wait there as she walked over to the guy. I watched her give him the money; he handed her the dope sack and hugged her.

On the way back Little Bit said, "Dee this is what you should start off with and then work your way up. With this amount, you should make one hundred and twenty five dollars. Maybe, the next time you can get one hundred." I told her while I was waiting on her to get the dope, I felt all eyes on me, and I was glad when she got back. She laughed. When we got back to the tent she gave me the bag of dope and I counted twenty five rocks, each rock was five dollars. While I was counting my rocks, Little Bit said, "You might just make one hundred dollars." I asked her, "why?" she said "Because you might smoke some," with a laugh. "You can sell your nickel rocks for a ten to the truck drivers." "Oh really!" I responded. I was learning a lot; I was glad to have Little Bit there for me. Little Bit stayed on a street no one else was on which made things even better. She told me I could sell outside the tent or go to the Texaco station. "I don't feel good so I'm going to lie down for a while," she later added.

As I sat outside and sold my dope people passed by asking for Little Bit. I told them she was sleep, but I had something. Everything was going great because they bought from me. I had no problems! Even Jello came and got twenty five from me. This was fun and easy; now I have a hustle, and I didn't have to worry about trying prostitution which terrified me. I hated the fact of having sex for money and I hoped to never have prostitution as an option.

When I finished selling my rocks, I made one hundred and fifteen dollars, and that's because I saved two rocks for myself to smoke. As I looked up I saw Rob coming. I hurried in the tent to put my money up and went back outside while Little Bit was still sleeping. I sat outside the tent and talked with Rob. After a while he asked me to go to the produce market with him. I didn't ask why he was going to the produce market, but I saw he had a big bag with him. I waited outside as he went in the store; he didn't come back out with the bag. When we got back to the tent, Little Bit was gone. So we sat in the tent and smoked my two rocks, and he gave me ten dollars.

I was getting to know a little about Rob, so I thought. He began to come around every day and I started hustling in the street with him. Little Bit didn't like the idea of me spending so much time with him. She always told me to be careful hanging with Rob and to not allow him to get me in to any trouble. I enjoyed hustling with him because it was new. I liked moving around and meeting people. It gave me no time to think about my problems, but I could never get use to the things I saw happen in the streets. Just the other day, I saw a man get beat to death. It made me sick and I couldn't understand why no one said anything. They just watched, and I couldn't do anything, but I did say something to Rob. He said, "Girl you don't stop nobody's fight or call the police." I was in tears, I could not sit there; it was too hard to watch so I told Rob, "lets go." I finally understood what Little Bit meant when she said these people don't have a heart. I said to myself then, "Lord please don't let my heart harden like theirs."

The days were going by fast, and I was forgetting the reason I was down there. I was getting caught up and didn't know it, but I always had the girls on my mind. I would tell myself that they were better without me right now, and I knew they were safe so I had nothing to worry about. I missed them so much and would try not to think about them. It was very hard, and it made me smoke more. Time began to get intense; I was out in the street a lot. Rob and I would stay up for days and I didn't see Little Bit for days.

One day I was selling dope at Rob's place waiting on him to get back from the produce market; I realized it had been two days without sleep or food. All I've been doing is hitting dope and moving around. I was scared to go to sleep at Rob's place. I also needed to go check on Little Bit. When Rob got back I told him that I wanted to go. I needed some rest and I needed to let Little Bit know I was alright. He said okay and walked with me. As we walked, he asked if I was ready. Rob was my teacher just like Little Bit.

When we got to the street it was full of people. There was an ambulance there and two police cars near Little Bit's tent. So we both ran to the tent. They were bringing Little Bit out of the tent. I was so scared. Rob asked was she okay and the police just said move back; they would not tell us anything. After the ambulance left, I sat down on the curb. Rob said, "Dee do you want to get your things out the tent. You can stay with me until Little Bit gets back." I got up off the curb saying okay. I didn't want to stay there by myself. I went inside the tent, and then Rob said, "Why don't you take the tent and sit it by me." I said, "No!", and he said, "But Dee she would want you to take it." I answered no again, and went inside my tent to gather my things. I wanted the tent to be there when she got back. While gathering my items, I found a jar full of money. The money was wrapped with a rubber band around it inside the jar. I put the money in my bag. I was sure glad Rob was outside the tent when I found the money.

When we got to his tent, I went inside and sat thinking about Little Bit; I wanted to cry. I felt scared, got up, and went outside. Rob was talking to this guy in an eighteen wheeler parked across the street. Rob saw me come out of the tent and walked over and asked me for help because he was short on money and needed to get a dope sack. I asked how much he needed and he said, "No Dee, see that truck that is parked across the street, well he wants a girl." I said, "Man I don't do that." "Girl you are a mega star go get that money," he responded. I said no. Then he got mad at me and said, "Bitch all I do for you." I said, "What, you haven't done any more for me then I have done for you." Then he said, "If you don't get your black ass out to that truck you can leave." And I did just that. I guess he thought since Little Bit wasn't around and I was a newbie he could talk to me any type of way and I would listen. He didn't know me; I would fight a man. So, I gathered my things and left.

While I was walking, I heard him call my name but I didn't look back. I kept walking until I hit 7th street where the hotel was. I still heard Rob in the back of me calling my name. I felt him getting closer, and by the time I turned around he grabbed me by my neck and said, "Bitch, give me some money!" I said, "I'm not giving you anything punk." By this time, I heard someone say, "Rob, leave her alone." It was Tony and he said, "Dee, are you okay, what's the problem?" Rob said, "She owes me some money." I said, "No, I don't; he wanted me to get into this truck, I told him no and he got mad." Tony said, "Man, you need to quit that old shit. Dee I believe you, this is how he gets down. Plus he likes beating up on ladies. Stay away from him. Man, go about your business and leave her alone unless you want some of me." Rob turned to walk away, and says, "Dee, this is not over."

Tony looks at me and says, "You didn't go home? Girl you still look good. Where are you going?" I told him to the Rivers Hotel. So he said, "Okay I will walk with you. It looks like you need a bodyguard." I laughed and he asked if I am sure that I'm alright. I replied, "Yes!" and gave him a hug while telling him thank you. When we arrived at the hotel, Tony said, "Okay. Dee if you need me, you know where I'm at." I said, "Okay" and walked inside the hotel.

91

After getting up stairs, I counted the money I had taken from the tent and the total came to three hundred and fifteen dollars. So I put it away in my bag for Little Bit. I wondered how she was doing. I didn't know her real name to locate her at the hospital. After, I decided to go downtown to buy a few items. When I got to the lobby, I thought about what Rob said, and I knew I had to watch my back. As I walked I continued to turn around and look behind me just in case he was waiting for me to come out of the hotel.

On my way back I decided to stop and get me a sack of dope to keep my money coming in. I didn't want to be without or depend on anyone else. I went to the guy that Little Bit went to on 5th street. I didn't know his name so I just went over to him and said hi and told him what I wanted. He said, "Damn girl, what's your name?" I told him, "Dee, I'm Little Bit's friend." "Okay, I heard about her and I'm so sorry to hear that she died," he responded. I was so shaken I could have fallen to my knees. I didn't let him know that I didn't know Little Bit was dead. He asked me what I said I wanted, I told him, and he gave me a sack. I handed him the money. He said, "It gets better Dee, so come back." I said okay and asked him his name? He said, "Money." Later I found out, Little Bit died of stomach cancer.

On my way back to the room, I overheard two guys talking about Rob and how he had just got busted for dope and stolen goods. I could not believe what I heard but it put a smile on my face. I would never wish for anyone to go to jail but at least now I could relax a little.

Chapter Six

Back on 7th street in front of the hotel, I saw this guy beating up on this girl. He held her down on the ground with his foot in her chest taking her money. Everybody was standing around looking; nobody would help her. I didn't say anything, but I felt so bad for her. After he got her money he left. I helped her up and said, "Sorry he took your money." She said, "It's alright. He's a jerk and mad because I broke up with him. What's your name?" "Dee, What's yours?" I replied. She said, "Pam," then asked, "Didn't I see you down from McDonald's selling?" I told her yes. She asked me what was I doing now. I told her the same thing, trying to get my dope sack sold. Then she asked if she could help me because she needs the money. Of course I said yes. Then she said she wanted to get a room so she can get off the street. I told her I needed to first go up stairs to put my bags up. She said, "Okay, I will be right here Dee."

I didn't have time to process the fact that Little Bit was dead. After putting my bags up, we started to sell. I told Pam to only watch my back, but she was sending people that wanted dope to me. She really helped me out a lot and we finished fast. So, we went to get another sack. When we got back Pam said, "Dee let me go in the store, before we get started. I need some cigarettes." While I was waiting on her this sort of tall and slightly bow legged (also cute) man walked up to me and said hello. I responded with hi. Then, he said he had been watching me all day. He asked my name? I told him Dee. Then he said, "no disrespect but girl you got a body. What are you doing?" I said, "selling," and he responded, "Well, how are you doing with that?" I said, "good." Then he asked where I was staying? By this time, Pam was coming out the store so I said, see you later and I walked away. He said, "Hey Dee, where are you staying?" I didn't say anything. Pam asked,

"Is he talking to you?" I said yes. So she asked, "What's wrong with you, he's cute." I said, "Pam let's just make this money girl." She replied, "okay."

When we finished, we decided to buy another sack. After that one, I promised myself I'm going to rest. I still haven't had any sleep for two days. However, I wanted to make enough money to help Pam out; so she can get off the street and maybe her own sack. I remember when Little Bit was there for me. I sure missed her because she had taught me a lot. After we finished the last sack I gave her one hundred dollars and paid twenty dollars for her a room at the same hotel I was staying in. Then, we went up stairs to our rooms to rest. I told Pam we would start back at ten o'clock, it was around six o'clock then. Pam said, "okay Dee I'm not sleepy, but I'm going to lay down."

When I got to my room, I laid across the bed and wondered how I got here. My life is just a mess I thought. I feel like I'm on a dark one way dead-end street trying to survive until I find my way back home. It's so hard to explain! I just don't know. I'm so ashamed and I can't bare to face my family. I wish I knew how to deal with these feelings. I love them and miss them so much. I guess it's my pride because I never asked or wanted this lifestyle. I never wanted to sell drugs, it just happened. Somehow along the way I got caught up. Little Bit had warned me. It's funny because I can remember when I got my first job in high school. I worked at StarKist Tuna Factory in the city of Long Beach, Ca. When I finished school, I went to work for the Air force station under a government contract. I started as a file clerk and moved up to a document control clerk. I later moved up to the Administrative Receiving Clerk position and decided to go to school to become a Legal Secretary. After graduation, I worked at a law firm. I even modeled part time and was in beauty pageants. I was first runner up and I won miss talented. I have always had good jobs. I am a good person; however, I made wrong choices. I don't know why I can't stop smoking. I do know that I am not the same person I use to be; I have really changed. I don't know how to go home without feeling like a loser. With all those thoughts, I finally fell asleep but I didn't sleep long.

When I woke up it was eight thirty, and I was very hungry. I got up and washed my face. While I was washing my face, I remembered the money in the jar. Anyways, I went to Pam's room to see if she wanted to eat, but when I knocked on her door she didn't answer. So, I decided to go by myself. As I walked down the hall on my way outside, I passed a room with the door open. I heard someone say "Dee." I doubled back and it was the guy I was talking with in front of the store. He said, "Dee, I asked you, where did you stay, and you didn't say, but see I found you any way.

My name is Switch Blade." I couldn't do anything but laugh. He said, "Come in, what are you doing?" I told him that I was hungry and on my way to get something to eat. He said, "Really, I'm hungry too, so can I walk with you?" I said yes. "What do you want to eat Dee?" he asked. "I got a taste for some chicken, is that okay?" I asked. He replied yes. So, we went to Kentucky Fried Chicken, I was so tired of McDonalds.

After getting our food, we walked back to the hotel. I looked at Switch Blade and told him that I was going to my room to eat and would be back outside to sell soon. He asked what time, and I said about an hour. He asked, "Would you like to sell with me?" I said, "Yes, until Pam gets back." Then we both went to our rooms. I agreed to sell with him because I didn't want to be out there by myself. After I finished eating, I counted my money and went back to Pam's room to see if she had made it back.

But she had not, so I went to Switch Blade's room. He was sleep, but he got up and we went outside to sell.

While we were selling, I looked up and saw my first cousin Annese. She is Bobbie's (my mother's sister) daughter. I was so shocked and surprised to see her. I called out to her; she looked up, saw me and we both walked to each other and hugged. I asked her what she was doing down here. She said she had an apartment down here and pointed to the building that sat on the corner across the street from the hotel. We talked for a while and she asked me a lot of questions. Some I wasn't ready to answer. She told me that my girls missed me and will be here this summer. I was so glad to hear that. I told her that I talked to them and they are always on my mind, but that I hate to call sometimes because I only cry and if I stay on the phone too long they would hear me crying. Plus I hate telling them the same thing, that I will be home soon. Then she asked me what I was doing? I had to tell her. I asked her where was she going? "I'm going to the store and to get me something to eat," she replied. I showed her where I was staying and said I'll see you later. By that time, Switch Blade had come over to us. I introduced them and then Blade and I went across the street continuing to sell.

After a while, I saw Pam. I asked her where she had been. She told me that she been in the back of the Texaco Gas Station and "it was hot up there; the police were everywhere," she added. "Dee, I couldn't sleep, but I can now." I said okay and I continued to sell. Blade came to me and said, "Dee let's take a break." We went to his room. When we got there, Blade said, "Sit down Dee, do you know I have a son?" I asked, "How old?" "He is seven years old," he answered. Blade added, "I have not talked or seen him in six months. I really feel bad; so I am going to see him tomorrow." He started to tell me funny stories about him and his son which had me laughing.

After Blade's stories, I told him that I had three girls and started telling him stories. I told him that my oldest daughter came in the bathroom where I was cleaning, and she asked me why birds run from you when you try to get close to them? I didn't know what to say, because I didn't like telling my girls anything so I told her to wait until I finished cleaning the bathroom and I would tell her. I was trying to think of something that made sense to her. But before I could think of something, LaQuita was back saying "Momma, I know why?" I asked, "Why, baby?" She said, "Because we are bigger than they are." I said, "You are so smart." She said, "I know momma." And she left smiling.

I also shared the story of my middle daughter Raquel asking me when her titties were going to get big. Now, she was only three years old. So I told her if she ate all of her food, then goes to sleep when I tell her to go to bed; when she gets older they will get big. So she said okay. After four days passed, Raquel said, "Momma I'm eating all of my food and I go to sleep when you tell me to go to bed and my titties still not getting big." I told her to just keep doing what I said. I told Blade, I remembered looking at my mother when Raquel said that and my mother said, "That's your daughter," and started laughing. I told him I missed my baby Erika. She always stared at me with her big eyes, smiling.

He asked me if I go see them. I said no. "Do you call them?" I said, "Yes but not in a while." So he asked why? I told him that I was tired of telling them that I will be home soon, and plus I end up crying before I get off the phone. He said Dee why don't you write to them. How come I didn't think of that (I thought to myself). I said, "Thank you Blade, that's just what I'm going to do. But I don't have any paper." Blade said, "No problem." He went down stairs and got me some paper and handed me a pen. He told me I could buy a stamped envelope from the store on the corner. I said, "cool" and started to write my letters.

After I finished, I went to the store and then to the mailbox on the next corner, I felt so much better. When I got back, Blade was sleep. So I locked his door and went to my room. I really needed to call my mother to tell her I was mad at her because I had been putting it off. I felt that she left me at the wrong time. I was so mad at her, but I wanted her to be happy. I don't think she understood how sick I was. I was sick, broken and in a very dark place. We all know you can't fly with one wing. I love her so much. Maybe she was showing me tough love and just felt I needed to grow up. Maybe she didn't understand because she never had a drug addiction; cigarettes are all she's ever smoked. So, I called my mother.

After hearing her voice I told her I loved and missed her. I could not tell her I was mad because I didn't want to upset her. We talked for a while, I told her I was alright, and I was going to get myself together. Before I got off the phone, I asked her if she had all three of my girls. She told me no, that Erika's father stayed in California and he didn't want her to leave the state because he had jurisdiction over her. I sat there for a while after I got off the phone, feeling hurt. I didn't want my daughters to be separated. I knew I had to get out that room because I was crying and mad at myself. I couldn't sit there depressed; I had to get out and move around. There was nothing I could do about that situation at the moment.

I went back to Blade's room. He was awake and we went outside to sell. I stopped selling to check on Pam. Pam was still asleep, so I went back outside with Blade. After selling for about two hours, Blade and I sold out. So I went with him to get more dope. We sold that pack, went up stairs, and called it a night. After that, I slept well for a while. When I got up, I went to get something to eat. On my way back, there was a guy standing in front of the hotel wanting something to smoke. He asked if I was selling. I told him yes, but I had to re-up. I started to go and see if Blade had re-up yet, but I didn't. I told the guy to come go with me to re-up.

We walked two blocks over, and I told him to wait here on the corner. I walked to the guy Blade and I went to last night named Dallas. The guy gave me a twenty-dollar bill, and I told him I will be right back. I walked up to Dallas and I said, hi. He said, "Hi I remember you, what do you want with those pretty eyes?" I told him and gave him my money. He gave me a sack. I walked back to the corner, gave the guy his dope, and he walked away.

Then I heard someone call my name. So I turned around and saw this guy named Trouble. I met him when I was out and about with Rob. I walked back to see what he wanted. He said, "Say Dee, you do have something right?" "Yes, what's up?" I said. He said, "Dee I got some new clothes so can we make a trade." "Let me see them," I responded. He said, "Go in the tent." I saw some pants and a jean jacket. So I said, "Okay Trouble, this is what I want. Now what do you want?" He said, "Dee give me a nickel rock." I said, "okay". Before I came out the tent, I heard trouble say, "Dee, one time!" then he adds, "Dee there is three more cars coming and it looks like there stopping here. Oh shit, Dee they are." So I hid my dope in the pant's pocket I had just got from Trouble. Before I made it out of the tent, the police pulled back the opening and said, "Here she is." I could not believe this; I had made a direct sell. I'm on my way back to jail. Before they put me in the police car, I told Trouble to go to the Rivers Hotel and ask for Pam in room 33 and tell her what happened and to try and get my things out my room. The police was pulling off with me in the back seat, but Trouble heard me and said okay. When I got there, they fingerprinted me and booked me for direct sell. The day I went to court the judge gave me six months and told me if he saw me in his courtroom again I was going to prison.

I didn't try to call anyone but my father. My father put money on my books. He asked me if I was tired, and told me I needed to pray. He said he was praying for me and wanted me to get back to my girls. "They love you so much and they worry about you. They're getting big now and it won't be long before they won't need you," he stated. I said, "yes daddy, you're right" and got off the phone because I started crying. I'm so tired of crying. I knew what my father said was true; that made me cry even harder. But it didn't make it easier for me to go home because I want to finish what I started, then I will feel better about myself. Annese told me that the girls would be here for the summer and I'll be here in jail, so I won't get to see them.

When I got out, I went to the hotel to get a room with the money I had left on my books. I went to Pam's room and was hoping she was still there. When she opened the door, she was surprised and gave me a hug. She told me that Switch Blade got busted two weeks after me. Pam also said her friend that just got out of jail whom was in court with Blade said the judge gave him two years. She said, "Dee, Blade was so mad when you got busted, and so was I. I missed you. Mrs. Chin let me get your things out of your room and I still have them. Dee I spent your money, but I can give you fifty dollars now and I will pay you the rest later today. I just came back from getting a sack and I haven't made any money yet. Are you okay?" I answered, "yes."

Pam continued with, "Let me tell you about Tony. Girl, Tony got shot in the head. Girl, Tony is gone. You do know Tony right?" "Yes I do Pam what happened?" "Dee I don't know, but I heard he got into it with this guy at the Texaco Station and the guy pulled a gun on him." I told Pam how I met Tony when I first got down here. When I stopped to rest and Jello started talking crazy to me, and how he came to my rescue. "He just helped me out with Rob, when Little Bit died. He will be missed," I said. I asked her what she had been doing? She said, "The same ole thing." Then she said, "Wait Dee I'm not finish, the police found at least four girls dead. I know they found one of the girls behind the dumpster. And girl it is so scary out there, I don't go no where by myself. I'm so glad you're back. And Dee, one girl was pushed out the window; she was on the ninth floor at the Cecil Hotel. Oh, and that girl Jello is in the hospital." "What happened to her?" I asked. "Dee, they say she got AIDS," she replied. "Oh my God!" I added.

After hearing all that, I was ready to go to my room. Pam helped me with my bags she held for me. Getting in my room, Pam gave me some of my money and we sat and talked longer. Then she left and I went to sleep. I slept the whole night. When I got up the next morning, I was so hungry I didn't even shower. I washed my face, brushed my teeth, got dressed, and went to Pam's room to see if she was hungry. Before I could knock, she was walking up behind me. She had been to the store. I asked her if she had ate; she said no, then I asked if she wanted to go to the mission for breakfast. And she said, yes. So I waited on Pam to go in her room and come back out.

While I was waiting, I thought about momma. I needed to call her. I said I was mad at her because she left me, but I was mostly mad at myself. On our way downstairs, I saw Mrs. Chin, the owner of the hotel, she said hello and told me that she had some mail she had been holding for me. Right away Pam said, "That's Switch Blade." I asked, "You think so?" We were wrong. I looked at the letters and got so happy; it was from my daughters. I couldn't wait to get back from breakfast to read them. I felt sort of funny eating at the mission because I haven't ate there since Little Bit died. Also, I had money and didn'thave to eat here.

On the way back from the Mission, we stopped to get a dope sack for me. You would think I learned my lesson after going to jail. But, I messed up my G.R. checks when I went to jail; so now, I have to sell to keep my room. Anyways, we got the sack and headed back to the hotel. I couldn't wait until I got up stairs. After reading my daughter's letters, I had to call them. So, I went outside to the phone booth. I called and my stepfather answered the phone and said they were gone with my mother. He said, "How are you doing Delores?" I said okay. "Well call back and I will tell them you called." I said okay. He said, "Take it easy." Then, we both hung up.

I looked up and I saw this guy name Danger. He said, "Dee you're out, come take a hit with me." He would buy dope from me, so I did. We went to this parked abandon car around the corner that he slept in. When we got to the car he got in on the passenger side and I got in on the driver side. He started to mess with his pipe changing the screen as I stared out the window. All of a sudden, I saw some spirits. No joke, I tried to duck down in the seat and hide behind the car that was parked in front of me. But they came out from around the car where I could see them.

They got really close and just disappeared. I told Danger that I changed my mind and I got out the car. I went back to the phone and I called my Aunt Lacy. I said, "Hi Lacy, this is Delores." She was happy and said hi. I start telling her about what just happened to me. She asked, "Delores are you high?" I told her that I haven't had anything to smoke. "I just got out of jail yesterday. I haven't smoked, but I was just about to." She asked me was I scared when I saw the spirits. I answered no, but surprised. She said, "Why didn't you ask the Lord what he was trying to show you?" I said, "I don't know. I was hoping I wasn't going crazy." My aunt told me to come home. She said, "Delores, I'm praying hard for you every day." I got off the phone when I saw Pam. I didn't say anything to her because I didn't want her to think I was crazy. Pam said, "Dee what's wrong? Why are you looking like that?" I said, "Nothing are you ready to sell?" But those spirits stayed on my mind. I had never seen spirits before, and I didn't understand why I saw them.

After selling all day, I went back to the phone booth, and I called my mother. She was there so I talked with her for a while. I didn't tell her about the spirits because she would have said I was crazy. I asked to speak to my girls. I told them that I was sorry I didn't get a chance to see them this summer. They both wanted to know why I was in jail. I told them that we would talk about it when I saw them. LaQuita asked, "When is that?" I said, "Soon." I told them to keep their heads up, to walk and talk like ladies, to stay in church, and study hard in school. They both said, "Okay, I love you momma." Raquel added, "But when are you coming home?" I said what I have always said "soon baby." I asked to talk back to their grandmother. I told my mother I loved her and to please not worry.

After getting off the phone, I went to my room to clean it up. When I finished, I headed back outside. I closed my room door and saw this guy at the room right next to mine. He looked up at me and said, "Hi, do you know where I can get some dope?" "Like what?" I said. He said, "a rock." I said, "yes." But I didn't tell him I had it. I told him to go in his room and I will bring it to him. Then I asked, "How much do you want?" He said, "a twenty rock, do you want my money?" I said no, "I will be right back." I went in my room after he closed his door. It's a good thing he stopped me because I had forgot my dope sack. I got my dope sack and I pulled four rocks out and took them to him. I knocked on his door and he answered and lets me in with a pipe in his hand. So I said, here and asked for the money. He gave me a twenty-dollar bill. Right away he put one rock on his pipe and started to hit it. Then he looked up at me while blowing the smoke out pointing to the rocks. I wasn't sure what he was trying to say with smoke in his mouth. After he finish blowing the smoke out his mouth, he said "take a hit." I said, "okay." I pulled out my pipe from my socks and I picked up a rock and put it on my pipe. I put the pipe to my mouth and before I could hit it, he had picked up the last two rocks and put them on his pipe. He blew out his smoke, and said, "Girl, if you give me another hit like this, I will give you all my money." I stopped and took the pipe out of my mouth and put it in his mouth. Then he hit it and blew out the smoke. He said, "Go get me a drag queen." I said, "Oh no, you said if I give you another hit, you would give me all of your money." So he started to pull money out his pocket and I stopped him. I told him I was just playing while laughing. He gave me his money anyway and again said go get him a drag queen.

I knew a drag queen down the hall named Summer, but I really didn't talk to him. But I took a chance and went to his room. He was there and I asked him if he dated. He said yes. I told him that this guy wanted a girl. So he went to his room with me. Before I left them, he asked him how much money he wanted. He said, fifty dollars. So he looked at me and said pay him. I started to say what; but I was nice and paid him. Then I told Summer I was next door in my room if they needed me. I went to my room and began to feel bad. I felt bad because I had never done anything like this. "Who am I?" I don't know anymore. (I thought) I have changed so much. After thirty minutes passed, I heard a knock on my wall. I knew it was them; so I went next door. They were finished with their business. So, Summer thanked me and handed me ten dollars. I said, "Thank you, but what's this for?" He said, "for coming to me." I was surprised. He left and the guy looked at me and said, "by the way my name is Stan. I come here once a month and when I come back I will look for you. You are so different.

I can trust you, thank you. And what is your name?" I said, "Dee." He took his shoe off and gave me a hundred dollar bill. Then said, "Now you have all my money" with a laugh. Then, he gave me a hug and he left.

I went to my room and I sat on the bed. I was trying to understand why I felt so bad. I knew it had to be because of what I had done. I didn't believe in homosexual activities but I have to say this; I made three hundred and ten dollars in one hour. I felt bad but happy with the money. I started to think about how much I have changed. My lifestyle has become an addiction. When will I get home? It seemed like I was so stuck and there was no way out. I wanted to overcome it by myself. I tried to stay busy to not think about home, but it was hard not to. I didn't know which way to turn. I said I wanted to go home but really didn't know how. Why is that? I knew I would figure it out.

With the money I made, I decided to buy me a phone. I went by Pam's room to check on her. When I got to her room, she said she was about to check on me. I told her I had made some money and was going to buy a cellular phone, which would make it easier to call my girls. I asked her to come go with me. She said, "Okay Dee, but let me pay you the rest of your money." I told her to keep it. Then, we went downtown and I bought me a phone and three pair of pants. On the way back, we stopped to get something to eat. When we finish eating, we went on to the hotel, but Pam stayed outside to sell.

I went to my room and called the girls to give them my number. My mother answered the phone; so I gave her the number and she called the girls to the phone. They were in the next room watching television. I gave them my number and talked to them for a while. I called my aunt Lacy and my father to give them my number as well.

When I was on the phone with my father he said, "So you're out of jail, I'm glad. Now are you tired of them streets? I'm still praying for you and I know you will come home when you get tired." He continued to talk and ended with I love you and I said, "I love you too." When we hung up, I went outside where Pam was and watched her for a while; then decided to take a walk. I walked to the Texaco Station. When I got there, the police was there and they had some people against the wall so I kept walking. After walking for a while I heard a car behind me. So I turn around and the car stopped, and oh my God, it was my brother Tony. I couldn't run. He called out to me and I went to him. He said, "Hi Delores, what are you doing? Get in the car." I did, we began to talk and he asked me to come go home with him. I told him not now, but I was. He begged me. I saw tears in my brother's eyes and I had to get out the car. He kept trying to talk to me. But I walked away. In my heart I wanted to leave with him, but it seemed like something was stopping me. It hurt me to see the tears in my brother's eyes. Tony eventually drove off, and I walked back to the hotel my heart very heavy.

I got to the hotel, went upstairs, and I received a call from my Aunt Lacy saying my father was really sick. I had just talked to him, I thought.

She said, "You need to come see him and fast." For a minute I sat still, I got off the phone, got some clothes ready, and got Pam to go to the Greyhound bus station with me. Then, I called my Aunt Lacy back, and told her I was on my way. She said, "Call when you get here, and someone will pick you up."

Chapter Seven

When I made it to Oakland, Ca., my cousin Connie was there to pick me up. After I got to my Aunt Lacy house, Joyce and her boyfriend Richard came over to take me to see my father. Joyce is my mother's youngest sister. When we arrived at the hospital, we found him in his room lying in the bed. I said "Hi daddy!" and he looked at me. I kept talking to him, and finally realized he didn't know who I was. We sat there for a while talking anyways. While we were there, the nurse came in and said, "he was asking for Delores, but now his cancer has spread to his brain." After the nurse left,, we sat there a little longer before we left. I held his hand and he kissed me. Then, I told him I loved him and will be back.

I went back to my Aunt Lacy's house, and told her about my visit with my father. Lacy said, "Delores you know your daddy had this cancer for a long time and the Lord has been good to him." I said, "Yes I know. It was just hard to see him like that." She told me to go lay down for a while. So, I did and when I got up she said I could go eat. Then, she asked me if I wanted to go play bingo with her and Annette. Annette is my aunt Lacy's daughter. I told her yes; so, after I ate we went to play bingo.

When we got back Lacy called my mother. I talked with her; the girls were not at home. When my Aunt Lacy and I got off the phone with my mother, we sat and talked all night on into the morning. After two days passed, I was ready to leave. My aunt wanted me to stay; it was so hard to say no, but I didn't want to live off her (that was my excuse). The truth was I wanted to smoke. So I left, and two weeks after I got back, I got a call from my aunt saying that my father had died. She also told me she heard his family was sending his body to Homer, La. for the funeral. When I got off the phone I called my mother. My mother said, "Delores I just heard, are you alright?" I said, "Yes, are you going to the funeral?" She said, "Yes, to take the girls."

After hanging up with my mother, I decided to lie down, but before I fell to sleep all I could see was my father's face. He was staring at me from his hospital bed. I loved him and he didn't even raise me. I didn't find out he was my father until I was eighteen which was very hard on me. I was raised by my stepfather Janatha who passed away in 1975. After I cried for a while, I soon fell asleep. When I woke up, I laid there in bed for a while. I thought about how I wanted to go home, but I couldn't seem to go. It was like something had a hold on me. The sad thing is I enjoyed my lifestyle.

Some years have passed and I'm still downtown. One day I go to Pam's room; she's not there, so I go to get a dope sack. Walking back a car pulled up to me, I figured he wanted something to smoke. I made a big mistake, and I got into the car. Before I knew it, there were police cars surrounding the car. I figured I was busted for suspicion of prostitution. Off to jail I go, I was so mad at myself. Why did I get in the car, I kept thinking. I knew better. When I got to jail, they searched me, and found my sack of dope. So now, I have a dope charge and I'm scared. When I went to court, it was the same courtroom and the same judge. He told me if I showed up in his courtroom again he was going to send me to prison. The judge said, "so soon Layton," and he sent me to prison for three years.

All I could do was cry; I was so scared. I was in the county jail for two months before they sent me to prison. I went to prison in December of 2003, and I went crying. When I got to prison, they changed me from my county clothes into their prison clothes. They gave me a number, and sent me to the nurse whom asked me all sort of questions. They wanted to know if I took any medication.

They checked for lice and then showed me where I would be sleeping. They also told me I would see a counselor in the morning.

After I ate breakfast the next day, I was called to see my counselor. She told me that I would only be in prison for thirteen months. I have to go to school or work. But in my case, I will work and go to a drug class. I said okay and went back to my dorm and met some of the girls. Most of the girls had been there for a while. This was an ugly place filled with women. I wanted to call my father, but he was gone. I didn't want to call my mother but I knew sooner or later I would have to. I started working and went to school the next day. I worked from 7 am to 12 pm and went to my drug class from 12 pm to 2 pm. We had to be up at 7 am to have breakfast and had to be in bed at 10 pm when the lights went out. My job was cooking in the kitchen.

Two weeks after I was there, I called my mother. She said, "I knew something was wrong. How long do you have to be there?" She asked for the address and said she would send me some money. Then, she gave my daughters the phone. They said, "Hi momma" and told me they were doing good in school, I didn't even have to ask them. I told them I love them and be sure to write me. I got a letter the next week from them, and they continued to write me. I was so happy they were writing to me; it made the time go by fast, but not fast enough.

I went to church every Sunday and promised myself when I got out I was not going back downtown. I said I was going home. One day my counselor called me to her office. She asked me if I was interested in a drug furlough. I asked her what was that? She said, "That's when you can finish your time on the street in a drug program, and you would parole from the program." I told her, "Yes, I would like that." She said she would put my name in for the program. Then added, "Layton, if you try to leave the program before your parole date, you will get a warrant put out on you for escape and that's another year. So be sure you stay in the program until your parole date. Layton, when you parole, they will give you two hundred dollars; this is gate money. You will have to report to your parole officer until you get off parole. And if you don't report to him, you will get a violation and that's a warrant." This really seemed like a lot.

I believe I have learned my lesson now; this was hard for me. They tell you when to get up, when to go to sleep, when you can eat, what you can and cannot do, and when you can use the phone. I will be glad when my time is over. Weeks have passed and today I received some mail. I was so happy it was from my daughters and my mother. My daughter LaQuita told me that I was going to miss her high school graduation. Time goes by so fast. I never meant to be away from my daughters this long. When I left them to go to the drug program downtown, I knew I made the right decision, but it turned into the wrong thing because I got caught up and stuck while makings all the wrong choices. I really thought I knew what I was doing. I got curious; I guess I needed to know what Skid Row was all about. I just got caught up. I was really trying to get out of the mess I made without my family's help.

One day I almost got into it with this girl, but a girl sitting next to me said, "don't do it because you would only get more time added to your time." It was hard not to say anything, but I didn't. She looked like a man. We were at lunch when this happened. I wanted to leave but I couldn't; we all had to leave at the same time in a line. I was told she was a lifer, just bitter, and wanted to mess up my time. Prison is like the streets, but worse. What was I thinking, when I was living on the streets acting like I had no family. In prison everything became real clear. I was crazy; I felt if I didn't get myself together something bad was going to happen to me.

When I got to my dorm, I saw clean linen on my bed and made my bed up. I remembered it was Saturday because there was no work or school. I was in the dorm with six women who talked all the time. This one particular day they began talking about their first love. I couldn't believe they were acting so calm like they were at home. They were all laughing and having fun. One girl looked up at me and said, "Delores, that is your name right?" I said, "yes." She asked, "Do you remember your first love?" I said, "Yes, I sure do. His name was Victor, and we were together for two years. He then left me for another girl breaking my heart. One of the other girls said, "That's what I'm talking about. I should have shot the nigga." I said,

"What?" Someone said, "Yea, she is in here for cutting off her man's penis." All I said was oh my goodness. Then some girl asked me what I was in for. I told her and another girl said me too. Then the rest of the girls start telling what they were in for. We talked until the lights went out.

The next day, I went to church. The church service was good; I really enjoyed the choir. After service, I went outside to the yard for a while and then I watched television. It's getting close to me leaving to go to the program. My mother said she would send me a dress out box. I continued to work and go to my drug class. One day I was in the television room I met this woman who was seventy years old. She killed her boyfriend; he had been beating on her for a long time. She said she was twenty years old when she came in. I thought, oh Lord they need to let this women go. I really doubt she would come back. I talked to her a little while longer and she told me she had a son that visits her. About an hour before bedtime, I told her good night.

Weeks have passed and it was time to go to the program. I had to go to another prison for transportation to take me to Santa Fe Spring to the drug program called the Phoenix House. I was so happy; it's almost over. I have gained so much weight. I was so glad to be out of prison. In actuality, I'm really still in prison because I can't leave until my parole date. The program is nice. We all have jobs in the house. There are different levels of the program, and we have to work are way up through the levels. My job was in the kitchen, again. That's why I'm so big they keep putting me in the kitchen.

One day, I grew courage to call my brothers; I wanted to let them know I was in a program and I wanted to see them. My brother Anthony and I were always close. I knew I needed my family around especially since my head was clear. The next week my brother Anthony and my nephew Marcus came to visit me. I was so, so happy! My brother said he was proud of me and now he would be able sleep. They told me I looked good, that my mother and daughters would be down here for Christmas, and they can't wait to see me. This was a good day.

Chapter Eight

A few months have passed, and I am leaving the program soon. I decided to talk to my case manager to see if I can stay longer, and go to sober living; but I don't think I'm ready to leave. To tell you the truth I'm scared. My case manager said, "Delores this is a smart move. You need to get to the root of your drug use." After another two months I went to sober living and I felt so good and proud of myself. They placed me in a two-bedroom condominium with another lady that had been here alone for a while working while living in one of the rooms. A younger lady and I were placed in the other room together but thankfully the rooms were big with large walk in closets. The bedrooms were upstairs, each with their own bathroom and down stairs included the living room, kitchen, washer, dryer, garage, and exercise room. I really like this place.

The lady that ran the place was nice. I had to go to N.A. meetings once a week, and for my food I would make a grocery list and they would get our groceries, but we did our own cooking. It was really set up nicely. For income they took me to the G.R. building to re-apply. When we wanted to leave the house for more than two hours we had to put in for a pass unless we were out looking for jobs. We also could put in for a pass for overnight and weekends. My family was able to visit, but no overnight stays.

After two weeks, I went to see my family. When I arrived at my brother's house everyone was there. I first saw my daughters, and they have really grown up. Wow! How time flies. We sat around, ate and talked. My girls are so pretty. My niece, nephew, and cousins all look grown. My other brother Janatha and his wife Sharon were there as well. I was so glad to see everyone; My mother, her brother Wilbert, and his daughters, LaTanya and Angie. We had a great time. My heart was filled with so much joy to be with my family. I didn't want to go when it was time for me to leave.

My brother Janatha took me back to sober living.
My brothers were behind me 100%; I have never felt better.
My sister-in-law Kathy gave me a bed comforter for
Christmas. My uncle Wilbert gave me money. My brother
Janatha gave me a phone and T.V. Overall; I received love
from my family, which meant more than any materialistic
gift. This was one of the best days of my life. After I got
back, I prayed and went to sleep. A few days later, my
mother and daughters came over to see where I was living
and to say bye. My daughters told me they were proud of
me.

After two months passed, I decided to go shopping
downtown. I thought I was strong enough, but I wasn't.
After getting down there I ran into this guy named Insane.
He said, "Where have you been girl? I haven't seen you in

a while." I said "I got busted, and I was in prison. From there, I went to a drug program and then to sober living." He asked me if I wanted a hit. I said no at first, then before I knew it I said yes and took a hit. Then I took another one and another one. Soon I started to cry and said, "Lord please get me back to sober living." And he answered my prayer. I got back and to my surprise they were testing everyone that went out on a house pass. I'm scared but I have to take the test.

The lady told me the test was negative. I was shocked especially knowing I just took a few hits. The devil was in my head telling me to run because they were getting ready to call my parole officer, and the lady told me the test was negative so that I would not think to run. I just knew they were lying and I was on my way back to jail for a dirty test so, I ran. I can't believe I messed up again especially with eighteen months being cleaned. I didn't know what to do. I felt I couldn't go to my family, and I definitely didn't want to go back downtown.

With the two choices, I ended back downtown looking for Pam. When I found Pam, I told her what happened. She said, "Dee, if they told you that your test was negative it was because they can't lie to you." That news made me feel even worse. The Lord answered my prayer, got me back and my test were negative. I let the Devil get in my head. I'm so stupid. Well, I know it's too late to go back. Pam said, "Yes Dee, I'm sure they have called your parole officer by now. They have to report your every move. What are you going to do?" "I don't know, I guess get a room," I answered.

So that's what I did, I went right back to my old ways. I had enough money on me to get a dope sack and a room. I realized that I had left some money under my mattress, and I couldn't go back for it. I was so mad at myself for messing up and leaving the money. I got out of there so fast, I wasn't thinking. After I got the sack, I didn't want to sell. So, Pam and I smoked the whole bag. I was crying while hitting. Pam kept telling me to slow down, but I wasn't listening. She tried to make me feel better, but it didn't help. She said everything that I had already said to myself. Pam soon left but said she would be back to check on me. I slept for the entire day.

The next day I didn't have any money for my room. I went outside to look for Pam and couldn't find her. I ran into this girl named Rhonda. She said, "Hey Dee!" I said, "Hi." "What's wrong?" she replied. I told her and she said, "Come go with me and let me see what I can do." We walked to her place; she had just got a dope sack. She sold dope and worked the street. I waited while she was counted her dope. There was a knock on the door, and she said, "Get that for me Dee." I answered the door and it was a client looking for her. Rhonda told him to have a seat. Five minutes passed and someone else was at the door. I answered the door; it was this girl by the name of Kathy. I didn't know her that well, but she said, "Dee, do you want to make some money?" She was really coming for Rhonda but saw she was busy. I said, "What do you mean? You know I don't date." She said, "But Dee all you have to do is flex your muscles. This man has a lot of money and a truck seat full of dope." So I asked why she got out the truck. She said she took a hit and she got spooked.

When we got to the truck, she introduced me to him. She said, "This is Dee and she wants to make some money." He said, "Get in, can you flex your muscles?" I looked at him and questioned, "Flex my muscles?" He said, "Yes," and then handed me sixty dollars, "Pull up your pants leg and flex your leg." So I did. This man looks scary, and I felt crazy flexing my muscles. He said, "Now flex your other leg," and hands me another sixty dollars. Next,

he had me flex my arm and gave me another sixty dollars. I

did it and told him that I had to leave. I had made one

hundred and eighty dollars and was ready to go. He said,

"Why, do you want a hit?"

I said, "No, this truck is smoky from you hitting, and

sooner or later the police is going to hit this block and I'm

not going to jail." He told me that the police was not

coming down this block. I said, "You don't know that." So

he asked if I knew where he could get a room. I told him

yes and took him to where I was staying, but I didn't tell

him that I had a room there.

He got a room and when we went into his room. I

told him I had to use the bathroom. You see the bathrooms

in this hotel are in the hallway on this floor. I didn't go to

the bathroom; I went to pay my rent. As soon as I walked

back in the room he said, "Can you do this?" He was

making his breast jump. I told him no. He said, "Well, I want you to do it but with your butt," and he hand me sixty dollars. I took the sixty dollars and I must have moved every muscle in my body until I did it. It was weird; he never asked me to take off any of my clothes. After I flexed my butt muscle, he hands me another sixty dollars and says, "Flex your leg again." I looked at him and he looks like he is looking right through me. I said, "You have some cold eyes." He said, "Why do you say that?" So I told him what I was thinking. He said, "Dee I'm thinking about taking you with me." I said, "What!?" and he said, "Yea, my cousin and I own a gym. Every month we pick two girls to compete in an exercise competition and whoever wins get six hundred dollars. So I asked, "How long do you think it would take me to get ready for something like that?" "Six weeks," he answered. (Jokingly laughing)I said, "Are you kidding? Man, all the exercise I have been doing today, I should be ready."

This man never smiled or laughed, he kept a straight face. I told him that he was being very generous, and when he goes broke I wasn't giving him any money back. He said, "I don't go broke." I replied, "Everybody gets broke sometimes.' He said, "Not me, I got more money in my truck". I told him that he shouldn't be saying things like that around here. Then he said, "Let me see you do your butt again," and hands me sixty dollars. I said, "No, I think I'm going to call it a day. Plus, it's getting dark. I have been with you all day and I'm tired." He looks at me and says, "You want to leave after you got my money?" I answered, "Man, I earned this money." I never knew his name, when I asked him he said it wasn't important. "Dee, you think God sent you this money?" he asked. "What?" I replied. Now, that was a question I didn't see coming. I asked, "Who did?" He said, "Me, the devil". I immediately was frightened. To myself, I said, "Oh shit, I'm on a date with the devil." I'm not sure what came over me but boldly said, "I don't care who you are; I know who the almighty is." Then I asked, "Do you believe in God." He began to turn his head. Shoot, I thought he was going to turn his head all the way around like in an exorcist movie. He didn't answer, so I asked him again. He put his hand in my face; it looked like he had a cross. So I was relieved. He asked, "Dee before you leave, take a hit with me with the lights out". I said, "No, why in the dark?" He said, "Open the curtains for some light." Then he hands me another sixty dollars. I was so ready to go so I said okay, but I didn't take his money. I said, "After I do this, I'm out of here." I went to open the curtains and I heard him say in a deep unfamiliar voice "don't do that." So, I turn around and see him coming to me. I ran around him and turned on the lights while running out the door. Before closing the door I heard him say, "Dee, I'll see you again."

I was moving so fast, I bumped into this guy name Busy. He said,

"Dee, are you ok?" I answered yes. He asked me if I had some dope for sale. I said, "No, will you go get me something and bring it to my room?" He answered yes. So, I gave him some money, and turned to walk to my room. He said, "Dee, what room are you in?" "Room 33," I replied.

When Busy got back, he said "Dee, when I saw you come out of that room you looked like you saw a ghost". I said, "I was scared". He said, "Why, what happen?" I told him. He then said, "Dee, I've seen many bad spirits down here; so he probably was the devil or a bad sprit. I said, "Man, please." Busy said, "Just listen Dee, didn't he tell you he doesn't get broke.

Well the Devil doesn't get broke". Then he scared me by

saying "Dee, I bet he didn't touch you?" I said, "No he didn't, I never took my clothes off, and we didn't have sex." "Well Dee, just because you didn't take off your clothes or have sex doesn't mean it wasn't a form of prostitution, because you did favors for money. Dee, the Lord will not bless you in prostitution. If the Lord blesses you, you will find it, earn it, or someone will give it to you. Yea girl, believe me it was the devil. Think about it, every time he gave you money it was sixty dollars, right? Girl, don't you know that's the beast number, 6. And didn't he tell you that it will take you 6 weeks to get ready for that exercise contest, and the winner of the contest will get six hundred. The devil always uses the figure six. Dee, the Lord had his hands on you. It's good you said you know who the almighty is because he was probably going to take you out the window. Didn't he say he would see you again? Yea, he probably will, but in a different form or fashion." I said, "Busy, you need to go." He said, "Okay Dee, but you better be careful." I said, "No, you're just crazy." He replied, "I know what I'm talking about Dee. Be safe." I told him, "Okay, I'm sleepy, so you have to go."

When he left, I took a hit and went to look for Pam. I couldn't find her, but I did run into Kathy. I asked her what that man's name was. She said he wouldn't tell her. "How much money did he give you?" I asked. She told me sixty dollars. When I looked up, he was standing across the street looking at me. I got scared, went to my room, packed my things, and left. In the midst of leaving, I found Busy and gave him my key to the room and I told him to find someone who needs a room and give it to them. He said, "Okay Dee, but where are you going?" I replied, "I'm getting the hell up out of here."

I went down the street to the Lyndon Hotel. After I got to my room, I laid on the bed to get some shut eye. I was on my back looking up at the ceiling, and began to reminisce about the times I didn't have any money. When I had messed up and had to go live on the street in a tent. I had really fallen on hard times. I remember being scared to sleep and being up for two days at a time without sleep. One day on the streets, I found ten dollars in my bag. I was able to buy me two nickel rocks. I cut them in half to make four nickel rocks. I gave this guy two rocks for a tent and gave another rock for a sleeping bag. I went to the mission to get two blankets.

After setting up my tent, I remember being hungry and tired. I was too ashamed to get in the food line for the homeless that the church sometimes set up on the street. After sitting for a while watching, I got up and got in line. Later, I felt so bad. It was one of my lowest moments; I ended up smoking my last rock. Sitting in my tent about to cry, I heard someone say, "Dee, this girl say she is your daughter." I came out of the tent and saw my oldest daughter LaQuita standing in the street and my niece Tonisha in the car. I was so happy to see them but I remember wanting to take off and run because I looked so bad. I didn't want my daughter to see me like that. My pants were filthy, I looked a mess. LaQuita made me get in the car and go with them to my brother's house. Before I left, LaQuita gave me some of her pants to change into and some money. She was on her way back to Louisiana and because of my pride I was on my way back downtown.

After reminiscing, I ended up falling to sleep. When I got up, I got me a bag and began to sell. But of course trouble always finds me. While selling, this young guy tells me he was the only one who can sell dope out of this hotel. I told him that it was enough money for all of us. He responded, "I'm not playing, you better not sell anything else." Of course, I continued to sell. One night after selling, I was cleaning my room and someone knocked on my door. Something told me not to answer the door, so I went to the door and looked through the peephole. I asked, "May I help you?" He said, "I want something for fifty dollars." The guy had a hoody on and I knew better not to open the door but I did. I opened the door and let him in. He came in and said, "Do you have something for fifty dollars?" I answered yes. I went to get my dope sack while he acted as if he was getting his money out his pocket. When I turned to count out ten rocks, he grabbed me by the neck and started chocking me. I couldn't do anything; I tried to grab him but I couldn't. I felt myself going out, so I said Lord please don't let me go like this. Something said play dead, and that's what I did. The man dropped me like a piece of trash and started to walk around my room looking for money I figured. Every time he stepped over me, I hoped he didn't look down at me while I was laying there trying to control my breathing. When he left out of the room, he didn't close the door. So, when I got up to close the door, I poked my head around the door, and he was standing there by the door and saw me. I couldn't close the door fast enough; he pushed the door back on me, came back in the room and began to chock me again. This time I went out.

When I came to myself, he was gone. I began to cry and started to look around my room. He got all my dope but didn't find my money. He chocked me so hard I could barely talk. Later I found out that the guy that told me to stop selling in the hotel paid this guy to come in my room and scare me. When Busy found out what happened to me. He tried to give me a gun, but I told him to take it back. "I don't need it." Hell, I couldn't even call the police. I'm on parole with a warrant for leaving the program, and I definitely wasn't going back to jail.

For the next few days, everything was done on the down low until I figured out what I was going to do. One day I heard Busy calling me through my window. So, I went down stairs to talk to him. He said, "Look Dee you were right, you didn't need a gun." He showed me homeboy getting busted. After, I sent Busy to get me another sack of dope. When Busy got back he said, "Dee, you are so bold. Most men are scared of that dude. Didn't I tell you to be careful when you left the hotel? That devil is still out here." I paid him and said, "Bye Busy." He started to laugh and said, "Bye Dee, I love you."

Chapter Nine

The next day, I was on my way to get something to eat. I never carry a purse around with me outside, but for some reason I did that day. This guy saw me walking and hollered out his window. He asked me if I wanted a ride. I went to the car and said, "Hey I'm going to McDonalds." I consented because I knew his face. When I got in the car, he said "So, what have you been up to Dee?" I said, "Nothing much," wondering how he knew my name. He drove passed McDonalds and I said, "Where are you going; you're passing McDonalds?" He said, "I know I have to take my girlfriend the door key because she is locked out the room." So I said, "Where?" He said, "At the Cecil Hotel." Before I could say okay, he drove passed the hotel. Then I said, "Let me out," but he kept driving. He didn't say anything or look at me.

I tried to open the car door to jump out, but he put his foot on the gas pedal to go faster. I was so scared and I didn't know what to do. I hoped a light would catch us, but he knew what he was doing. He did not let one red light catch us. He turned off the main street on to this wooded neighborhood. You can tell it was a rich neighborhood by the type of homes and large green lawns. I tried again to jump out but he sped up. He made a sudden stop, jumped on top of me, and said, "Open your legs bitch." I fought against him while tightly holding my legs together. I immediately remembered my scissors I kept in my purse. So, I reached for them in my purse. When I got the scissors in my hand, I was too scared to use them, but mind quickly went to survival mode. It was either me or him. I went down hard on his back and again on his head. He said, "Bitch you're trying to kill me." He reached for the scissors while I felt for the door handle. I opened the door and fell out the car back first while clenching my purse. He stabbed me in my leg and caught me over my eye before I hit the ground. I hit the ground and rolled down the hill. I got up and ran back to the main street. I could hardly see due to the blood running from my eye.

A taxi cab stopped for me and asked if I needed to go to the hospital. I responded, "No, but I will pay you to take me home. I stay on 7th street and wall." He asked, "What happened?" I told him and he replied, "Well, you need to call the police." I told him that I could not and asked if he would please take me home. We pulled to the hotel and I walked straight to my room.

The next day, I stayed in my room sleeping until that evening. I later went outside to sell. This guy walked up to me told me his name was Jam. He told me that he sees me a lot. He asked, "Why are you out here? You don't look like you should be down here. You are so pretty and seem so nice. You don't remember me do you?" "No," I answered. He replied, "About two days ago you gave me a dollar in the store, and now I want to pay you back. Your name is Dee right." I said yes. Then he asked me again, "Why are you down here?" I replied, "Why are you down here?" He began laughing and said, "I'm not trying to be nosey, I am just trying to get to know you." I asked, "Why?" "You're not going to make it easy for me, are you?" he replied. "I heard what happened to you in the hotel; when you got chocked out and robbed. Dee, why don't you go to the mission?" "I don't want to," I answered. Jam said, "You would be safe there at the mission." "I'm alright," I replied. "Do you have your ID and social security card?" he asked. "Why are you asking me all these questions Jam? No disrespect, but it's none of your business." He answered, "Okay, I'm just trying to help you." "Why?" I asked. "Dee I really don't know, but I'm going to leave you alone for now." He left and I started back selling.

Later that day I saw him again. He came up to me and hands me a flower. I said, "Not you." "Please don't tell me you don't like flowers Dee," he responded. I questioned, "You don't give up do you?" He answered, "If you let me give you twenty dollars, take you to get your ID and social security card I just might. I said, "Are you serious, but who said I didn't have them." He asked, "Well do you?" I told him I need a social security card, but I have my ID. He said, "Cool then we can go and get that." I said, "Okay, meet me in front of the Lyndon Hotel at 9 am." He said, "Okay, thank you." What am I getting into now, I thought to myself. The positive thing was I had been planning to get a card, but never made time.

Later I saw Pam; I asked her if she knew this guy name Jam. She said, "Yes, he's cool. He is always by himself. I've never seen him with a girl." "Well is he gay?" I asked. She answered, "I don't think so, why?" "I just want to know if he is a cool person," I said. She said, "It's more to it, what's up?" I said, "There you go being nosey." She said, "Oh it's like that Dee." I began laughing, told her how I met him, and what we were going to do tomorrow. "He said he has seen me around in the streets, but I didn't tell him that I saw him too." Pam said, "That's real nice of him Dee. He must like you or see something in you like I do." I said, "Yea right, let's go take a hit." On our way to my room, Pam said, "Dee, you act like its wrong for someone to want to do something for you. You are a good person and you care about people, so what is your problem. Thank the man and be nice." "I will thank him; I just want to know his expectations. I know it's something," I replied.

Before we got to my room, we ran into this guy that bought dope from the both of us. He said, "It's my birthday and I want to get a fifty. Do you want to go to my spot and smoke with me?" Pam wanted to go so I went with her.

This guy stayed in the basement of an abandoned building. He had it fixed up like a living room. It was really weird; we stayed there for about thirty minutes. While we were there he talked about hoes in the street. He said, "These hoes think they are something. You two look better than them and can get a man faster than they could any day." He looked up and added, "My mother was a hoe and she was my first piece of ass." Oh God, I thought to myself, it was time to go. So, I looked up at Pam, gave her the eye and we left.

Later in that week, I ended up over there by myself because I was out selling and it started raining. His spot was the closest covered place. So, I went over to his spot and asked him if I could stay until the rain stopped. He said yes. When the rain slacked up, I left. He wanted me to stay but he was talking and acting weird. Three weeks later, Pam told me that the police found out he was staying there and made him leave. They boarded the building doors and windows up. She said, "He moved under the bridge by the railroad tracks. He invited this girl over; something the girl said made him mad, and he told her 'if she didn't get right, like the hoe she is, she will end up like the three girls he got buried next to his tent'. The girl must had left and went to the police department, and told them what he said. Dee, the police is there now, they've found girls buried next to his tent." When Pam told me this, I didn't want to believe it because I was alone with this crazy man. It could have been me in that basement. I should have been on my knee's thanking the Lord for having his hands on me, but I wasn't.

Remember Jam? Well he met me and we went to get my social security card and have been friends ever since. We did everything together. We enjoyed hanging out and shooting pool. Everyone thought we were a couple and soon we did become one. One day in his apartment, we were arguing about me going outside to sell. After we stopped arguing I had laid down on his bed and fell asleep. When I woke up, I went to the bathroom and noticed I was walking funny. It was hard for me to lift my right leg. Jam didn't notice at first but then said, "Dee, I believe you had a stroke, let's go to the hospital." I didn't want to go but Jam insisted. So, we went to USC Medical Center. The doctors ran test and lo and behold Jam was right. I had two minor strokes. The doctor said my right hip was lazy and that I would need rehab.

While in the hospital my daughter Raquel and my brother Janatha came to see me. I didn't even know Raquel had moved out here. I was glad to see my baby. I haven't talked to my family since I left sober living. I was happy they came to see about me and I ended up giving Raquel my jewelry to keep before she left. She told me my other daughter LaQuita was in school in Lafayette. After they left, my cousin's came to visit, but I couldn't figure out how everyone knew I was in the hospital.

Later that evening after everyone had cleared the hospital room Jam told me he wanted me to come live with him so that he could take care of me. He also expressed he wanted me to stop smoking. When I got out of the hospital I made sure Jam bought me a cell phone. I called my mother gave her my new number and Jam's address. I remember not staying on the phone long with my mother because I didn't want to answer any questions.

A few weeks later I decided to go to Anthony's (my brother" house to see Raquel. Jam made the trip with me so that he could keep an eye on me. He wanted to make sure I did not smoke. When we arrived, Raquel was the only one at the house. We sat and talked for a while and later Kathy, my sister in law, and Tonisha, my niece, along with Anthony came home. My brother was mad because Jam came along with me and he said I should have come alone. I explained to him I haven't been going anywhere alone since my stroke. My brother explained that I shouldn't have brought a man over there to visit and that it didn't look good. I fully understood and left crying though I didn't want to cut my visit short. Raquel walked with us to the bus stop and stopped by the bank and gave me some money before we parted ways with hugs and I love you. It felt funny taking money from my daughter. With all the years I have been on the street, I have never asked family for anything except from my dad when I was in jail.

About a week later, I got a call from my daughter, LaQuita. She explained that Raquel felt I was putting Jam before her and I explained that Jam was there to help me, but I called Raquel to make things right. My daughters have come back into my life and I could not lose them over a simple misunderstanding. One thing I could always say is that my girls always had each other backs. From then on the incident stayed on my mind. I put dope before my girls, but I am not going to allow a man to be before them. I worked on getting SSI disability to enable me to have some income while I planned on making my way back home and off the streets. I have put my daughters through a lot and I need to show them I care. I revealed to Jam that I would be going home soon to visit my daughter. He seemed unhappy for me. He asked when I was leaving and if he could go with me. I explained that I was not coming back. He looked sad, but I was still determined to get back home.

When my SSI was approved, I knew I was on my way home. Some type of income was all I needed to point me home. This way I won't feel bad or have to live off someone. I could probably be help. I was really getting tired of the streets. I treated Jam to dinner and a thank you card with my first SSI check. I needed to show him that I appreciated him for all his love and kindness. He is the one that helped me get off of drugs.

Every time it came down to making preparations to leave, Jam made it hard for me. He never wanted to hear about my future plans. One evening, he during a conversation he said, "If you are going to leave me just go." The next morning, he got up and went to the store and said he would be back. Two days later he was still not back; I contemplated on getting out in the street and searching for him hoping he would be back but also knowing it would be hard for me to get back into his apartment because I didn't have a key and I didn't want to leave the door open. I finally hit the streets but could not find him. When I arrived back at the apartment, the manager would not let me in. I went to the mission to get a bed but they were full. I tried to find Pam and couldn't. I knew it was time for me to go home.

Chapter Ten

I fell to my knees in the middle of the sidewalk and cried out to my heavenly father. "Father, I'm sorry, please forgive me. I need you and I can't do this by myself. I'm tired and I don't want to die out here. Father, if you help me get home; I will do whatever you ask of me. Amen." I got up with a few people looking at me. Most wanted to know if I was okay, I couldn't stop crying but told everyone who asked I was okay. After, I called my mother and told her what I wanted. She answered the phone, "Hey Delores, your daughter Raquel is getting married." I ignored her statement and said, "Momma I'm so tired and I want to come home, but where is home?" She said, "Delores call your brothers." I answered, "Okay." I didn't have much to say after that. My mother didn't understand I needed her and the girls not my brothers.

I didn't call my brothers because I was too ashamed. They tried to help me when I was in sober living and I let them down. I called my daughter LaQuita and told her the same thing I told my mother. She told me I could come live with her and bought me a one way ticket. I promised I would pay her back when I arrived there. I was so relieved when she said she would buy the ticket because if not I would have had to wait on my SSI check.

I left from downtown Los Angeles on the greyhound bus headed towards Shreveport, LA in October of 2010. I remembered when I sat on the bus I asked, "Lord, what took you so long?" I later thought about what I asked and answered myself, "No Dee, what took you so long?" All this time HE was waiting on me. LaQuita was there to pick me up. I was able to attend Raquel's wedding, which was very nice, and she seemed very happy. I was elated to be there with my girls. We were only missing my baby girl Erika.

LaQuita and I lived in an apartment in Bossier City,

La. We attended church at Praise Temple of Shreveport under Bishop Larry L. Brandon. Bishop Brandon is an awesome man of God. I learned from Bishop that my past has nothing to do with my future. He reminded me that people love me because of, and God loves me in spite of. Bishop Brandon has truly blessed my life and I have learned to love myself again. He welcomed me with open arms and the warmth of the members made it even better.

LaQuita served at the church and was later assigned to Praise Temple of Bossier which was closer to our home. Praise Temple of Bossier, my current church home, is under the leadership of Overseer Beryl I Cowthran. Pastor C (as the members call her) is a beautiful woman of God and I truly love her. Pastor Cowthran has taught me how to be patient and to trust and depend on the Lord. Trust me, when this woman of God speaks, she make my toes stand at attention.

I am a mother at the church (can you believe that). I write skits and poems for the youth at the church from time to time. I am also a church usher. My church family is truly awesome. I am so happy that the Lord has delivered me and I will never stop thanking HIM. HE loved me when I didn't love myself. I know that it was HIM who kept HIS hands on me. Every day I find something to thank HIM for and there is a continual praise in my mouth. You see the Lord had a plan, and it wasn't until I bowed down and cried out to HIM that HE got me home. If you are ever in the Shreveport/Bossier area please come join us for service. We are an oasis of love, where the doors swing open on the hinges of love.

I can stand firm today and say I no longer chase dope, I'm chasing after God. I am a proud grandmother. My first granddaughter, Azora Lee Cooksey, is so beautiful. I am finally able to truly enjoy my family. One of my daughters attend church with me, my oldest daughter is a First Lady (pastors wife), and I talk to my youngest often. Since I've made it home I've lost my stepfather. You see I could thank God right there. His passing was unfortunate but God knew just when to bring me home.

So if you find yourself in trouble and don't know where to turn, turn to my heavenly father. I know HE is waiting to hear from you. Try him! I did, and I haven't been the same. Please think about the choices you make, and stand against pride and shame. It only takes one decision to alter your whole life. May God bless you, I love you to life!!!

P.S. - Be on the look out for my next book "Stuck City Untold Stories"

FOLLOW UP

In 2015 on June 2nd I visited Skid Row after being encouraged to take a walk downtown to see how far I had come and maybe help someone along the way. I felt so blessed to see what the Lord had brought me out of because nothing down there had change. To look at the people and think about how I must have looked made me sad. I started to pray for the ones I left behind because I knew just who they needed. I know that God is the only one that can deliver them just like he delivered me. Before I got out of the car my goal was to talk one person into going home or getting help.

As I begin to walk my stomach was in knots and my nerves shot. I hope to make a difference in someone's life. I see this girl I knew back when, but she doesn't recognize me. So I walk up to her and say, "Yes you know me." She responds, "Dee!" while reaching out for a hug.

We hug and I ask, "How are you?" She said she was good. Then I ask, "Are you tired of living in the streets?" She answers, "It is what it is Dee." I told her it didn't have to be that way and asked why she hasn't went home? She said, "It's not easy." "I know it's not easy, but do you want to go home?" I asked. "Yes I do Dee," she responded. "You know the first step is to put the pipe down, pray and tell your father what you want. Ask HIM to help you get home. Then call your family." She said, "Okay Dee." Then I prayed with her and she began to cry. When she stopped crying she said, "Dee you look so good." I told her she can look good too, "what the Lord has done for me, he will do for you." Then I asked for a hug. I told her that I loved her and gave her my number to call me if she needed someone to talk to.

After leaving her I broke down and cried wondering if I could have said more to my friend. I hoped my presence said more than my words however I've said my final good bye to skid row and to my skid row family. I love you, and

hope the best to all of you. God Bless (bye)

Made in the USA
Middletown, DE
19 September 2016